PRAYERS
to Command Your Day

MARY TAYLOR

Copyright © 2015 by Mary Taylor.

Library of Congress Control Number: 2015906416
ISBN: Hardcover   978-1-5035-6374-2
        Softcover   978-1-5035-6375-9
        eBook   978-1-5035-6376-6

All rights reserved. No part of this book may be reproduced or transmitted in any form or by any means, electronic or mechanical, including photocopying, recording, or by any information storage and retrieval system, without permission in writing from the copyright owner.

This is a work of fiction. Names, characters, places and incidents either are the product of the author's imagination or are used fictitiously, and any resemblance to any actual persons, living or dead, events, or locales is entirely coincidental.

Any people depicted in stock imagery provided by Thinkstock are models, and such images are being used for illustrative purposes only.
Certain stock imagery © Thinkstock.

Print information available on the last page.

Rev. date: 04/24/2015

To order additional copies of this book, contact:
Xlibris
1-888-795-4274
www.Xlibris.com
Orders@Xlibris.com

Acknowledgement

I would like to thank God for the inspiration and revelation knowledge I received from all the teachings from my Pastors at Living Word Christian Center and World Outreach Ministry and my Instructors at Charis Bible College.

Scripture quotations are from the Holy Bible, King James Version (Authorized Version). First published in 1611. Quoted from the KJV Classic Reference Bible, Copyright © 1983 by The Zondervan Corporation.;

Scripture quotations are taken from the Holy Bible, New International Version®. NIV®. Copyright © 1973, 1978, 1984 by International Bible Society. Used by permission of Zondervan. All rights reserved. [Biblica]

Scripture quotations are from *The Amplified Bible*, Old Testament copyright © 1965, 1987 by the Zondervan Corporation. *The Amplified Bible*, New Testament copyright © 1954, 1958, 1987 by The Lockman Foundation. Used by permission. All rights reserved.

Prayers to Command Your Day

When you know that God hears you, you can have confidence that your prayers are answered. Whatever you ask in Jesus' name He will do it, John 14:14. God is not a liar. For all the promises of God in Him are yes and in Him Amen unto the glory of God. So, expect whatever you ask the Father in Jesus' Name and He will give it to you.

There is significance in names

Who you are is connected with your name

Your name symbolizes who you are.

When someone calls your name, what comes to a person's mind?

Is it a godly person or someone evil?

When you pray in Jesus' name, power, privilege, and opportunities happen.

You Pray In Jesus' Name:

1. Based on your **association** with Him

Jesus died for your sins, 1 Corinthians 15:3

2. Recognizing that He is your **access** to the Father

Your access is through the death of Jesus Christ, Ephesians 2:18

3. Because of the **authority** you have

As His child, joint heir, and redeemed saint, you should approach Him in boldness and confidence with your prayers. Romans 8:17

You have authority granted to you by Jesus Christ

4. In **agreement** with His will.

God will carry out His will in your life, Romans 12:2

When you accepted Jesus as your Lord and Savior, you were given the gift of righteousness. Righteousness is right standing with God. You are no longer an enemy of the kingdom but family.

The number one attack against Christians is to attack our gift of righteousness. Satan, (the enemy, the devil), has to get you to believe that you have to earn the gift of righteousness. He wants you to believe that you have to work for it.

But God tells you in the Word that you are established in righteousness which is permanent, everlasting, always there. The Word also promises that you will be far from oppression and fear. In the absence of fear, there is peace. Peace is simply security in the midst of hard times.

When you have peace, you can pray like this, "God I'm not going to trust in what the bank or doctor just told me. I'm righteous in Your sight, and You are making a way where there is no way. I'm in perfect peace with no panic in my heart because You control my destiny. My confidence is in You." Peace also means nothing is missing or broken; it means you are whole.

The only thing you are lacking is knowledge. You are destroyed for a lack of knowledge. Hosea 4:6

By the time you finish reading this, you will believe that answered prayer is your assurance because you are the righteousness of God.

It's time to start approaching the throne of God like a table that is laid out with everything you need. You are His child, so you go to the table and receive whatever is in your heart. God's not going to give you a serpent when you want fish!

Think this way: "I'm taking myself some healing today. I'm taking myself some deliverance too. I'm taking prosperity. I'm taking a double portion of that. I'm going to do it because I'm the righteousness of God! I can do it! I am a child of God and He hears me." So, come boldly (like children with assurance/confidence) to the throne of grace to obtain mercy, and find grace to help in the time of need.

"By the acknowledging of every good thing which is in you in Christ Jesus," causes your faith to work. You see, every good thing is in you in Christ! You've already got it! And He said He would never leave you nor forsake you Heb. 13:5. So, instead of praying "Lord, just be with me this week, if it is Your will, for Jesus' sake" or "O, God, where are You? God, could You just love me? I don't feel the love of God," **instead pray**, "Thank You Father that You'll never leave me that You're always with me. Thank You for Your goodness." You just start acknowledging the good things that the Word says are in you, and then your faith begins to be effective. You'll start seeing these things manifest in your life. That is so much easier than begging God for something that is already done!

God has already done His part. When Jesus died on the cross, He said, *"It is finished."* Just believe and receive.

I saw some little boys playing near the edge of a pond; they were throwing sticks into the water. One of the boys slipped and slid into the pond. The water was not deep so he just stood up to get out but as you can imagine, he was wet. You know what I discovered when he fell into the pond? He did not turn into a fish. He was wet, but still human (obviously).

When you fall into sin, or doubt your righteousness, it's the same as believing water can turn you into a fish. It's outrageous to believe that! As a redeemed son or daughter of the Lord Jesus, you never turn back into a sinner; you're always the righteousness of God.

The day you made Jesus your Savior, your old sin nature died. Now you have a new root; you are a new creation producing a new kind of fruit.

God has given us dominion and power over the earth because of the finish works of Jesus.

Your assurance and confidence for answered prayer, peace, and eternal life comes from the finished work of Jesus.

Your life should be a continuous process of prayer which is conversation with God

Your life will become evident that you have a relationship with Him.

Satan's job is to get you to doubt that relationship and God

A few months ago I was having pain in my knee, I quoted 1Pet 2:24 but I was still in pain. I asked God, "What's wrong?" The Lord said you're fighting to get healed instead of fighting because you are healed.

You might say, "I don't see the difference." There's a huge difference! If you didn't understand the difference, then I can guarantee you, this is one of the main reason you aren't receiving from God. We all need to get a revelation of this. Jesus has already provided everything we will ever need. We're blessed with all spiritual blessings, all of them!

The Lord told me to command my body to line up with the word. Remember that Satan will try to tell you that it will not work when you do this. But I use the word to stop any pain Satan tries to cause me, just like I would take a painkiller to stop the pain. The pain is coming less frequent with very little intensity. Satan just wants to see if I really believe what I'm saying. This is just one of those spiritual battles you have but you must know that you already have the victory. I rather say the word every day instead of taking a painkiller.

God loves you, whether you feel it or not! His love has been poured in your heart- in other words, in your spirit. And His love isn't conditional upon your good actions, or holiness. You've got to start from this place that "God has already provided everything and if you don't feel His love, it's not that God didn't give it; it's that you don't realize what you have." When you know that you have something, it takes the struggle out of it. It removes you out of condemnation. It takes you out of a legalistic mentality of trying to earn things from God. It removes doubt. How could you ever doubt that you'd get something that you already have? It's really that simple.

But God wants us to pray:

1. To involve you in His work
2. To strengthen your faith
3. So you will live with a sense of dependence upon Him
4. So you will grow in an intimate loving relationship with Him
5. To bring us into agreement with His will, purpose, and plan

If you don't pray you will not have an intimate relationship with God

God will not force you, but will draw you to him.

Does prayer change things?

Your prayers change your relationship with God.

Don't just pray when things are going bad.

Pray without ceasing

God wants to bless you abundantly.

It is His will

Two assets to carry out His will

1. You can know His will because he has given you His Word
2. You can know His will because You have the Holy Spirit

Be Aware of your dependence upon Him

Have Assurance you will get the answers you need.

You will get exactly what you need

You need to begin to believe that things have happened that you can't see, taste, hear, smell, or feel.

You can believe that there are television, radio and cell phone signals in the atmosphere, even though you can't see them. You know that all you have to do is take a cell phone, turn it on, and receive signals to make a call or check your email and you'll see that those signals were there the whole time. You need to begin to apply this to spiritual things. You can't just limit this concept to just the physical realm.

There is more going on than just what you can perceive with your five senses.

Make the most of the next 367 days. When you pray, come to the Father based on your *association* and *authority* and recognize that you have *access* to Him through Jesus Christ.

Everything we do is creating a future. Rest *assured* that you are being responsible for your future as you command your day and you will have whatsoever you

Make the most of the next 367 days. Expect your life to change. Expectation is to watch with intense anticipation. I hope these prayers cause you to seek a deeper relationship with God. Hope is an intensely anticipation of good. Expectation is the foundation of hope. My question to you is: Who or what sets your expectation level? Let God's Word set your expectation.

Where you start is not where you will end up.

If you don't know the Lord, I invite you to get to know Him. Christ died not only to forgive your sins but to bring you close to Him into everlasting life. I believe that these prayers will cause you to desire to also have communion with Him. Each day let the prayers you read inspire you to focus on the one thing that matters most; how God sees you. Prayer is not a monolog, it's a dialog. God is not a genie to just get ones' needs met or telling Him all your problems.

Prayer is saying back to God what He has said about you; particularly in the new covenant. Always say that you are bringing into the physical realm what has already been done in the spirit realm. Meditate on the prayers and receive everything already given in Christ then praise and thank God for manifestation, then testify to someone of God's goodness in your life.

When you pray, come to the Father based on your *association* and *authority* and recognize that you have *access* to Him through Jesus Christ. Everything we do is creating a future. Rest *assured* that you are being responsible for your future. as you command your day and you will have whatsoever you say.

Prayers to Command Your Day

Day 1- *"For God has not given us a Spirit of fear, but of power and love and a sound mind." 2Timothy 1:7*

I declare I have power over fear and the enemy. I am Your beloved. You have perfect, unconditional love for me, which "cast out fear". I have the mind of Christ. I thank the Holy Spirit and Your Word, which helps me to think from Your point of view, I am bold as the Lion of Judah, In Jesus' Name Amen.

Day 2- *Therefore if any man be in Christ, he is a new creature: old things are passed away; behold, all things are become new. 2 Corinthians 5:17*

I declare I have been "re-generated". God's grace and love has changed me. I walk in His unmerited love, favor and power. I have new mercies every morning. I experience love, joy, peace, and victory. I am overflowing with blessings from God, in Jesus' Name, Amen.

Day 3- *"These things I have spoken unto you, that in me ye might have peace. In the world ye shall have tribulation: but be of good cheer; I have overcome the world". John 16:33*

I declare I have hope in the face of trials and temptations! I am so happy and thankful that Jesus has overcome the world and given me hope and a future. Jesus, because of Your power, love, and sacrifice, I too overcome the world! You give me joy and initiative to keep moving forward. You are my greatest inspiration and encouragement, and I love You Jesus, Amen.

Day 4- *"For our light and momentary troubles are achieving for us an eternal glory that far outweighs them all"* 2 Corinthians 4:17

I declare I do not fear the path that God is leading me on. I embrace it. For God is bringing me down a path to ensure the reward of my inheritance, in Jesus' Name Amen.

Day 5 - *Moreover the law entered, that the offence might abound. But where sin abounded, grace did much more abound: That even as sin has reigned in the death, even so might grace reign through righteousness unto eternal life by Jesus Christ our Lord. Romans 5:20-21*

Jesus, Your grace is greater than my sins. You are a God of many chances. When I turn to You, You turn my situations around until I see Your glory upon me! You are the One, "who redeems my life from destruction, who crowns me with loving-kindness and tender mercies." I trust You Jesus, Who qualifies the disqualified! You have done this for me that even when troubles are of my own making, they are neither final nor fatal. In Your Mighty Name, Jesus, Amen.

Day 6 – *"Forgive us as we forgive others." Matthew 6:12*

I declare I don't hold onto hurts, failures, mistakes done by me and what others have done to me. Lord You have not made me to carry these toxic emotions of unforgiveness. Here's the key – when somebody has hurt me, I don't curse it, I don't nurse it, and I don't rehearse it. Instead, I disperse it and Lord; You reverse it, in Jesus' Name Amen.

Day 7 - I will extol the Lord at all times; his praise will always be on my lips. My soul will boast in the Lord; let the afflicted hear and rejoice. Glorify the Lord with me; let us exalt his name together. Psalm 34:1-3

I praise You Jesus and give You honor for all the great things You have done for me. You deliver me out of all my troubles. I Glorify You Lord. I bless You at all times. Your praises are continually in my mouth. I exalt Your Holy Name. In the mighty Name of Jesus Amen!

Day 8 - *"Do not be anxious about anything, but in everything, by prayer and petition, with thanksgiving, present your requests to God."* Philippians 4:6

I declare I trust You Lord. You never leave me nor forsake me. You are not a man that You should lie. As I pray according to Your Word, You answer yes and Amen. You love me so much that even when I pray for a parking spot You give me the desire of my heart. Therefore I am anxious for nothing because You provide my every need, in Jesus' Name Amen.

Day 9 - *"Each man will be like a shelter from the wind and a refuge from the storm, like streams of water in the desert and the shadow of a great rock in a thirsty land."* Isaiah 32:2

Jesus, You have made me that kind of oasis for Christians and non-Christians. Those I come in contact with will become aware of their need for You. I will lead them to the shelter from the wind and their refuge from the storms of life. I might be the only Bible someone ever reads. I declare I am something worth reading. I declare I am available to be that shelter for a non-believer. I also declare what Isaiah 32:3 states *"Then the eyes of those who see will no longer be closed, and the ears of those who hear will listen"*, In Jesus' Name Amen.

Day 10 - *"Jesus Christ is the same yesterday, today, and forever"* *(Hebrews 13:8)*

The same Jesus who went around blessing others with 12 baskets full of leftovers, a net-breaking, boat-sinking load of fishes, and who never impoverished anybody, has empowered me to succeed in life. The same Jesus who went about doing good has caused good to explode in my life. The same Jesus who went about healing the sick and never giving anyone sickness keeps me in divine health and protects me from harm. Jesus You have empowered me to live the high life—the abundant life in which I see Your promises manifest! In the Name of the Father, Son, and Holy Spirit Amen!

Day 11 - *"His divine power has given us everything we need for life and godliness through our knowledge of him who called us by his own glory and goodness. Through these he has given us his very great and precious promises, so that through them you may participate in the divine nature and escape the perversion of integrity in the world caused by evil desire"* 2 Peter 1:3-4.

Lord, Your very Word tells me that You have given me divine power to live this life as You want me to; to escape evil desires and to experience godly living. I draw strength from Your power and love and I practice moral discipline. I know You better, and have developed perseverance in doing Your will, and loving others. You get all the glory. In Jesus' name Amen!

Day 12 - Destruction and life are in the power of the tongue: and they that love it shall eat the fruit thereof. Proverbs 18:21

I declare my words have more power than I could ever possibly imagine, and it is those exact same words that I use to bring not only a great amount of praise to You Lord, but also dramatic shifts in my life for the better. I speak life. I bring light into the darkest of situation. By the authority given to me in the Name of Jesus I speak blessings over my life which will destroy and remove those mountains that I have struggled with. Amen!

Day 13 - *"casting down arguments and every high thing that exalts itself against the knowledge of God, bringing every thought into captivity to the obedience of Christ," 2 Corinthians 10:5*

I declare as a child of God, I don't live under mental oppression. Negative self talk does not roam freely in my mind where it can wreck my life. I actively take those thoughts as prisoners by the power of Your Word which changes my heart and mind. I bear the spiritual fruit of love, joy, peace, patience, kindness, goodness, faithfulness, gentleness, and self control, in Jesus' Name Amen!

Day 14- "And they were offended in him. But Jesus said unto them, A prophet is not without honour, save in his own country, and in his own house. Matthew 13:57

I declare I am committed to You Lord. My life of obedience will be an affront to the systems and people of this world. Thank you Jesus for bringing me out of a normal routine into a new revelation of You that impacts others. Jesus, You confronted the issues of Your day without fear of being rejected. I know that the deeper work You have begun in me may be a stumbling block to those around me. The words You give me may also be an affront to those around me too; but Your Word said, do not fear. Thank You Lord for using my words and life to draw others to You. I am Your ambassador. You have placed me here for this time to extend life to those who live in darkness, in Jesus' Name. Amen.

Day 15 - *May the Lord give you increase more and more, you and your descendants. Psalm 115:14*

I declare I don't limit God and I am ready for more increase in my life. Thank You Lord for being a God of every type of increase that's good and pure. Thank You for being for me and not against me. This world tries to limit me and put fear into my life, but God; You increase me! He that spared not His own Son…how shall He not with him also freely give me all things? I decree I experience supernatural breakthroughs in my personal life, my finances, and I see all the limits and barriers removed, In Jesus' Name Amen.

Day 16- Taste and see that the Lord is good; blessed is the man who takes refuge in him. Psalm 34:8

Not because I declare it, but because I've proved it in my experience, I've tasted, I've invited You Lord to come in and be an integral part of my life. And when I did that, I know You're good. When I taste something, I take it right into my mouth and it becomes part of me. And I believe that's why Your Word challenged me to "Taste and see." I won't let You remain external. You reside inside of me and You never leave me nor forsake me, in the Mighty Name of Jesus Amen.

Day 17- *"The Lord will surely deliver us; this city will not be given into the hand of the king of Assyria." Isaiah 36:14b-15*

The world is full of "Assyrian kings" who mock the idea of a living God who delivers. Without Your help, I would not overcome. Even when my back is against the wall, I pray; and because I pray, You move on my behalf. In fact, You move so powerfully that I do not have to fight the battle. I declare I see my enemies totally destroyed without one hand raised in battle! Father God, I will proclaim to the world that Jesus is the living God. He delivers. He hears my prayers and my enemies are totally destroyed. His answers are Yes and Amen, in Jesus' Name Amen!

Day 18 - "I count not myself to have apprehended but: this one thing I do, forgetting what is behind and straining toward what is ahead, I press on toward the mark for the prize of the high calling of God in Christ Jesus." Philippians 3:13-14

My past is not a hindrance but a help in moving me toward God's purpose for my life. Even though it meant pain and heartache, I have the Grace of God so that I do not let my past dictate my responses to the future. I move forward and avoid viewing the past; negative or the positive for more than what I can learn from it. Lord, You are always about doing new things in my life. You give fresh revelation of Your purpose in my life. I declare I do not live in the past. I declare I do not hold onto bitterness that may hinder You from doing new and exciting things in my life. You turn my wastelands into streams of water to give life and not death in Jesus' Name Amen.

Day 19 - But these people are robbed and looted. They are all trapped in pits and hidden in confinements. They have become prey with no one to rescue them. They have become loot with no one to say, "Give it back". "RESTORE". Isaiah 42:22

I refuse to be robbed by the enemy any longer. I declare RESTORE over my lost finances and opportunities. I declare RESTORE over my body and health. I declare RESTORE over my lost loved ones and broken relationships, "Father, I declare all this not based on what I have or have not done, but based on Jesus and His finished work at the cross. I declare all this in Jesus' name. Amen!"

Day 20-..."Hope does not disappoint BECAUSE the love of God has been shed abroad in our hearts by the Holy Spirit." Romans 5:5

I reject disappointment today! I declare I have supernatural hope and favor. My prayers have been answered. And my dreams come true; I awaken hope today, because the love of God has been shed abroad in my heart; and the Holy Spirit is flooding me NOW with Faith, hope and love, in Jesus' Name Amen!

Day 21- *You meant evil to me but God meant it for GOOD! Genesis 50:20*

I declare today that every plot and plan that people or the devil have formed against me, are interrupted by You Lord! They have turned in my favor. I release every hurt and betrayal from my heart, and forgive anything done against me. What the enemy sends to defeat me, You bend to complete me, in Jesus' Name Amen!

Day 22 - *Bless the LORD, ye His angels that excel in strength, that do His commandments, hearkening unto the voice of His word. Psalm 103:20*

I declare I receive supernatural might, strength and encouragement from You Lord and my angels today. Angels are ministering spirits sent to carry out the voice of Your Word. I dispatch my angels now to carry out the promises of victory, favor, health, and blessings in my life even now as I speak, in Jesus' Name Amen!

Day 23 - But his delight is in the law (the Word) of the Lord; and in His Word he meditates day and night. He shall be like a tree firmly planted by streams of water; whose leaf does not whither, who bears fruit in his season; and in whatever he does, he prospers. Psalm 1:3

Lord, I declare today that I am firmly planted by streams of living water. I continually bear fruit in my life. And everything I put my heart and hand to today shall prosper, succeed, and bring forth victory, in Jesus' Name Amen!

Day 24- *Beloved, I wish above all things that you would prosper and be in good health, even as your soul prospers. 3 John 1:2*

Lord, I thank You that I walk in divine prosperity today. My soul prospers in Your Word, producing divine health, life and energy in my body; and producing divine PROVISION, IDEAS & BREAKTHROUGHS in my job, finances, and business, in Your Most Holy Name, Jesus, Amen.

Day 25- *He himself bore our sins in His body; and carried away our infirmities, and by His stripes we were healed. 1 Peter 2: 24*

Lord, I command my body and soul to come in line with Your perfect will. Jesus, You took my sins, sorrow and sickness in Your body, and nailed it to the cross. I speak healing over my mind, my emotions and my body. I reject sickness and disease, and command it to leave me now, in Jesus' Name Amen.

Day 26 - *All your progeny shall be taught by the Lord, And great shall be their peace. Isaiah 54:13*

I declare my children are blessed! They are disciples of You Lord. They are taught by Your Spirit and the Word of God. They are sensitive to Your voice, and they are walking in the good, acceptable and perfect will of God, in Jesus' Name Amen!

Day 27- *Christ redeemed us from the curse of the law by becoming a curse for us—for it is written, "Cursed is everyone who is hanged on a tree"—That the blessing of Abraham might come on the Gentiles through Jesus Christ... Galatians 3:13-14*

Jesus, You delivered me from the curse of the law! The curse of poverty and lack has no right to remain in my life. I command lack to leave; and blessing and provision to come. I call forth every grace—favor and blessing to come to me in abundance today, so that I am fully furnished for every good work and charitable donation, in Jesus' Name Amen!

Day 28- *For if because of one man's trespass dying reigned through that one, much more surely will those who receive [God's] overflowing grace (unmerited favor) and the free gift of righteousness [putting them into right standing with Himself] reign as kings in life through the one Man Jesus Christ. Romans 5:17*

I walk in God's overflowing grace, unmerited favor; and the gift of righteousness in my life, today! Therefore I reign in life. Nothing in life reigns over me. I command pain, sickness, debt, demons and fear to bow down and submit to me today, in Jesus' Name Amen.

Day 29- *Anxiety in man's heart weighs it down but an encouraging word makes it glad. Proverbs 12:25*

Thank You Lord that I have learned that worrying or being anxious is not having faith in You. The Bible tells me that it's impossible to please God without faith. In faith, I give worry to You Lord and You give perfect peace whose mind is stayed on Thee. Thank You Holy Spirit for helping me not to complain about it, nor think about it over and over. I declare that I don't constantly talk about how hurt I am to other people, in Jesus' Name Amen.

Day *30 - "By day the Lord went ahead of them in a pillar of cloud to guide them...." Exodus 13:21*

Lord this is how I determine if You are giving me the green light to move forward? First, I gather facts. Fact gathering allows me to determine all the realities of a given situation. However, this does not ultimately drive my decision, but it can put a stop to it. Second, is the Holy Spirit guiding me in my decision? "If the Lord delights in a man's way, He makes his steps firm" (Ps. 37:23). Third, I ask, has my decision been confirmed? "Every matter must be established by the testimony of two or three witnesses" (2 Cor. 13:1b). This is Your way of keeping me within the hedge of Your protection. I declare I write my plans in pencil and give You the eraser in Jesus' Name Amen.

Day- 31 *I will cause those that love me to inherit substance and I will fill their treasures. Proverbs 8:21*

I declare I love You Lord because You first loved me. I decree that my treasuries are full. Thank You Father, for giving Your only begotten Son to die on the cross for me. That's true love, for love always gives, in Jesus' Name Amen.

Day 32- *If ye then be risen with Christ, seek those things which are above, where Christ sits on the right hand of God. Set your affection on things above, not on things on the earth. Colossians 3:1-2*

I declare I think on good things and not just the things of this earth. I know who I am in Christ. I am His ambassador on earth. I am dead to sin. I am hid with Christ in God. The same power that raised Jesus from the dead dwells in me. I forgive those who spitefully use me. The peace of God rules in my heart, in Jesus I believe Amen.

Day 33- *He that spared not his own Son, but delivered him up for us all, how shall he not with him also freely give us all things? Romans 8:32*

I declare Lord; You hear my prayers and Your answers are Yes and Amen. I pray Your will, (Your Word) and You hearken to Your Word. Therefore, what things I desire when I pray, I believe I receive them and I shall have them, in Jesus' Name Amen.

Day 34 - *For whatever things were written before were written for our learning, that we through the patience and comfort of the Scriptures might have hope. Romans 15:4*

I declare I have patience, comfort, and hope to get through trying times. I don't rely upon man's word; I go directly to the source of them – Your Word! It's my present help in time of need, in Jesus' Name Amen.

Day 35 - *No temptation has overtaken you except such as is common to man; but God is faithful, who will not allow you to be tempted beyond what you are able, but with the temptation will also make the way of escape, that you may be able to bear it. 1 Corinthians 10:13*

Thank You Father that my greatest failure and sorrow has become a powerful force in my life and the lives of others. My Valley of Baca (weeping) became springs for me and others. I have gone from strength to strength (Ps 84:6). I trust You Heavenly Father. You said in (Luke 10:19) That You have given me power over all the power of the enemy and nothing shall by any means hurt me. I declare I am in a place of victory, in Jesus' Name, Amen.

Day 36 - Delight yourself in the Lord and he will give you the desires of your heart. Psalm 37:4

I declare I delight myself in You Lord. Lord, You have given me new desires – godly desires, beneficial desires, the kind of desires that You have Yourself. You share with me desires that are beneficial in their fulfillment. And You satisfy all of those desires. I find real joy, peace, and satisfaction in my personal relationship with You, in Jesus' Name Amen.

Day 37- *Faithful is He that calls you, who also will do it. 1Thessalonians 5:24*

I declare that what You have called me to; I don't operate in my own strength. You strengthen and help me. I will fear not for You are with me. You never leave me or forsake me. You are my confidence, and You keep my feet from being taken, in Jesus' Name Amen.

Day 38- He heals the broken hearted and binds up their wounds. Psalm 147:3 Who heals all thine iniquities and heals all thine diseases. Psalm 103:3

Lord Jesus, I open my heart completely to You. Thank You for healing the wounds in my spirit—some which have been inflicted upon me by others; some which I have brought upon myself. As You well know, I have tried to deal with the pain from these wounds through self effort. You alone took care of these injuries. Just like the woman with the unstoppable flow of blood, I believe that just one connection with You released Your healing power to mend and heal me. You touched the wounds that have seemed incurable, and You healed them once and for all. I stand on the promise of Your Word. You have said, "For I will restore you to health and I will heal you of your wounds." I take You at Your Word. So I reached out and touched the hem of Your garment. I believe that from that moment forward, the flow of blood dried up, the pain ended, and complete healing came to every wound that I have incurred. Thank You, Lord Jesus. Amen.

Day 39 - I have come that they may have life and that they may have it more abundantly. John 10:10

Thank you, Jesus, for your obedience to the Father. Thank you, Father, for Your loving sacrifice. Thank you, Holy Spirit, for Your comforting guidance. Life is so much more with the hope I have in You, Lord. I am so glad that You have provided the way for me to have eternal life in Your presence--in a place where there will be no more tears and no more suffering; a place where there will be unimaginable joy, praise, worship, and peace. I also thank You for an abundant life here on earth. I praise You for Who You are and for what You have done and continue to do in my life, In The Mighty Name of Jesus, Amen.

Day 40- As the deer pants for streams of water, so my soul pants for you, O God. My soul thirsts for God, for the living God. When can I go and meet with God? Psalm 42:1–2 *NIV*

I praise and love You Lord and I lift my voice to worship You, Oh my soul rejoices. When I meet with You Lord that thirst in my soul is satisfied, and cannot be satisfied by anything but You. You said, blessed are they who hunger and thrust after righteousness shall be filled (Matt. 5:6). My soul loves You Jesus. You are so good to me, Amen.

Day 41 - *Bless the Lord, you His angels, who excel in strength, who do His word, heeding the voice of His word. Psalm 103:20*

Thank You Father for the angels that harkens unto Your Word I speak. I thank You that Your Word does not return void. You always answer yes and Amen to Your Word. You are not a man that You should lie. Thank You for loving me that You gave me Your Word as a source of help, comfort, and an example of Your love, In Jesus Name Amen.

Day 42- *He is ready to do "exceeding abundantly above and beyond all that we ask or think according to the power that works in us" Ephesians 3:20.*

I declare I come boldly to You Lord and ask for Your blessing. I have broken out of the confinement of my past and my pain which prevented me from asking. Jesus, You bore my pain so I no longer have to live in it any longer. The pain that defined my past no longer controls my present. I'm rising above my circumstances and living beyond my limitations. The Blessed Life begins with a choice. The Blessed Life begins with a BOLD prayer for Your blessing. With Your blessing in my life, I can do what You have called me to do, In Jesus' Name Amen.

Day 43 – *"as His divine power has given to us all things that pertain to life and godliness, though the knowledge of Him who called us by glory and virtue, by which have been given to us exceedingly great and precious promises, that through these you may be partakers of the divine nature, having escaped the perversion of integrity that is in the world through lust." 2 Peter 1:3-4*

Lord I thank You that I already have everything I need for life and godliness. Thank You for opening my eyes so I see the resources You have already supplied to meet my needs. Thank You for perfecting everything that concerns me. Thank You for Your promises, which are more precious than fine gold. I declare that the Holy Spirit does exceedingly great things through me, in Jesus' Name Amen.

Day 44 – *For I will be merciful to their unrighteousness, and their sins and their lawless deeds I will remember no more." Hebrews 8:12*

Thank You Father, for being merciful to me according to Your loving kindness and tender mercy. Thank You for blotting out all my transgressions and delivering me from all my sins. Thank You for creating in me a clean heart and renewing a right spirit in me. Thank You for never leaving me or forsaking me. You have done all these things because the full payment for my sins has been paid by Jesus on the cross. Thank You Jesus, Amen.

Day 45- *"I keep asking that the God of our Lord Jesus Christ, the glorious Father, may give you the Spirit of wisdom and revelation, so that you may know Him better. I pray also that the eyes of your heart may be enlightened in order that you may know the hope to which He has called you, the riches of His glorious inheritance in the saints, and His incomparably great power for us who believe..."* Ephesians 1:17-19

Thank You Lord for another day to get to know You more. Knowing You brings the only true meaning and purpose to my soul. Without You I am nothing. Spending time with You I experience a great time of refreshing which helps me to discover the real meaning and purpose for my life. I am so grateful for Your love for me. That You have a plan to prosper me and not harm me plans to give me a hope and a future. I love You Jesus. Amen.

Day 46- *"This is what the Lord says-your Redeemer, the Holy One of Israel: 'I am the Lord your God, who teaches you what is best for you, who directs you in the way you should go. If only you had paid attention to My commands, your peace would have been like a river, your righteousness like the waves of the sea"* Isaiah 48:17-18

I declare I seek You Lord today for what You want to teach me. I allow You to lead me, which ensures peace and righteousness in my life. I declare this is my unchangeable guarantee, in Jesus' Name Amen.

Prayers to Command Your Day

Day 47- "That all of them may be one, Abba, just as you are in Me and I am in You. May they also be in Us so that the world may believe that You have sent Me." John 17:21

Scripture tells me five will chase 100, but 100 will chase 10,000, (Lev. 26:8). There is a dynamic multiplication factor in unity of numbers. I declare that the Church is a hundred times more effective and unified group. That we have the same love for each other as You Father have for Jesus. That we are also drawn to each other with a common mission; that causes walls to fall down. The independent spirit is broken. Competition is destroyed. Satan's accusations are thwarted. Our love for each other is manifest to the world around us and lost souls seek this love and accept Jesus as Lord and Savior, in Jesus' Name Amen.

Day 48 - "He that is faithful in that which is least is faithful also in much: and he that is dishonest in the least is dishonest also in much." Luke 16:10

I declare Lord that Your voice has become clearer and clearer in areas of my life that are more complicated and harder to figure out. You are with me wherever I go and speaks to me in every situation. I am willing to do whatever You tell me. Problems increase in my life when I don't listen to You. So I listen with a humble heart to hear Your solutions. I thank You Jesus for being faithful to Your Word. Amen.

Day 49- "Do not let any unwholesome talk come out of your mouths, but only what is helpful for building others up according to their needs, that it may benefit those who listen." Ephesians 4:29

I declare I let the most encouraging and beneficial things come out of my mouth. Thank You for the strength and wisdom through your Spirit to think before I speak. The words that You give me are words of truth, words of light, words that are appropriate for the moment and the person or people who hear them. Those words are honoring to you, instructional, inspirational, motivational, and encouraging to others. You have given me the ability to be someone who supports others in whatever it is they need, so that they are lifted up and motivated to reach their potential… to glorify you… to be blessed and be a blessing. Thank you for hearing me, in Jesus Name, Amen.

Day 50- One day Jesus was praying in a certain place. When He finished, one of His disciples said to Him, 'Lord, teach us to pray, just as John taught his disciples.'" Luke 11:1

I decree I have learned that prayer is not just a five-minute exercise in the morning devotion time, but it is a vital strategic tool to discern and know Your will and purposes in my life. Lord You are almighty. My prayers are a covenant with You when I come together with You in prayer, preparing the way for Your will, and pray "with all prayer and supplication" (Eph. 6:18) to grant You the maneuverability to work in my life and others. I put prayer on the front lines, instead of making it an afterthought and I see renewed power in my life, in Jesus' Name Amen.

Day 51-To everything there is a season, and a time to every purpose under the heaven. Ecclesiastes 3:1

It can be so hard to wait for things, especially when I'm waiting for Your intervention for a special need. Thank You for Your peace to calm me down, to be patient, to remember that You have taken care of the situation in the right time; Your timing. You are all-knowing and all-powerful. I declare I put my trust in You. Thank you, Lord, for doing what is best for me, in Jesus Name Amen.

Day 52- "For God did not give us a spirit of fear, but a spirit of power, of love and of self-discipline." 2 Timothy 1:7

I declare I do not cower at the enemies' attacks. I do not weigh the risk of failure because I trust totally in You and I am more than a conqueror. I look at intimidations, accusations, and calamity that confront my very existence as training grounds. These training grounds are setting the stage for a great victory that will bring praise and honor to my heavenly Father for the greater victories to come, in Jesus' Name Amen.

Day 53- "Or do I make my plans in a worldly manner so that in the same breath I say, 'Yes, yes' and 'No, no'?" 2 Corinthians 1:17

1 Cor. 2: 16 tell me that I have the mind of Christ. Lord, I do not rely on my own intellect/mind for final decisions. I release all decisions into Your hands, in Jesus' Name, Amen.

Day 54-"See to it that no one misses the grace of God and that no bitter root grows up to cause trouble and defile many." Hebrews 12:15

The enemy of our souls has a very specific strategy to destroy relationships. I declare I will not allow the root of bitterness to be planted in my life. I allow the grace of God to cover the wrong. This grace prevents me from becoming a victim who will seek compensation for the pain. I don't lash out at the offending party. I move past the hurt, and a root of bitterness will not be given opportunity to grow, in Jesus' Name Amen.

Day 55 - "… I am not ashamed of the gospel of Christ, for it is the power of God to salvation…" Romans 1:16

I am not ashamed of the **good news** (gospel) of Christ, for it is the power of God to save me continually, in every area of my life. To keep me well, To preserve me from danger, To bless my finances, To bring well-being to my family, To renew my spirit, soul, and body. Because I am the righteousness of Christ I can experience the ongoing power of salvation each and every day. I proclaim this to the world, in Jesus' Name Amen.

Prayers to Command Your Day

Day 56-"Therefore My Father loves Me, because I lay down My life that I may take it again. No one takes it from Me, but I lay it down of Myself. I have power to lay it down, and I have power to take it again. This command I have received from Him." John 10:17-18

Thank You Jesus for this sacrificial, free will act which activates a response of love within me. I therefore commit my life to You. I give up my rights, privileges, and desires. I focus only on You. I give up my life in order to gain it. You sanctify and cleanse me by the washing of water by the Word that You present me to Yourself a glorious church not having spot or wrinkle but that I should be holy without blemish. When I am dead to self You give me the desires of my heart. I commit myself to laying down my life for You, in Jesus' Name Amen.

Day 57-"Simon, Simon, Satan has asked to sift you as wheat. But I have prayed for you, Simon, that your faith may not fail. And when you have turned back, strengthen your family." Luke 22:31-32

Thank You Jesus for being my advocate and intercessor. That when trials come they aid in my maturation process. I declare I pass the test because I know that You are with me. Thank You for the revelation that these trials are nothing but a divine set up to bring me into a higher level of maturity in my walk with You. It's not about me but how the experience can help me lead someone else to You, in Jesus' Name Amen.

Day 58- Behold, how good and how pleasant it is for brethren to dwell together in unity! It is like the precious ointment upon the head, that ran down upon the beard, even Aaron's beard: that went down to the skirts of his garments; Psalm 133:1-2

..., to know them which labour among you, and are over you in the Lord, and admonish you; 1 Thess. 5:12

Thank You Father for never leaving me or forsaking me. You are united with me. Thank You for the revelation that when I show up, You are there with me. Thank You for guiding me to God loving leaders with integrity. Today I will show Your character in everything I do, in Jesus' Name Amen.

Day 59-Therefore if any man be in Christ, he is a new creature, old things are passed away, behold, all things are become new. 2 Corinthians 5:17

I declare that the Lord has put a new spirit in me. He has given me the mind of Christ. 1 Cor. 2:16. I denounce allegiance with generational strongholds that impacted the way I viewed people and circumstances on a subconscious basis. The stronghold of fear, control, rebellion, insecurity, idolatry, pride, or bitterness, I command you to leave my mind and body, you are not welcome here, in Jesus' Name Amen.

Day 60-But seek ye first the kingdom of God and His righteousness and all these things shall be added unto you. Matthew 6:33

Every believer has gone through seasons of time in which it looked as if the Word wasn't working. But the difference between me and the ones with no root is my refusal to quit. I declare I see the kingdom of God manifested in my life. I keep speaking the Word and walking it out, no matter what it looks like to my natural senses which causes all things to be added to me, in Jesus' Name Amen.

Day 61-"'Come, follow Me,' Jesus said, 'and I will make you fishers of men.'" **Matthew 4:19**

Father, thank You for developing and preparing me for the work of the kingdom. Thank You for helping me through crisis in my life that will make an impact on the world. Finally, I thank You for the fruit bearing stage where Your power is manifested in my life so I shall become fishers of men like the world has never known, in Jesus' Name Amen.

Day 62-And it shall come to pass in that day, that his burden shall be taken away from off thy shoulder, and his yoke from off thy neck, and the yoke shall be destroyed because of the anointing. Isaiah 10:27

Lord, I want to recognize and honor You as my Messiah—the Anointed One who has forgiven me, released me from captivity, and chosen me for Your purposes. Thank You, Lord, for the pouring out of Your grace upon me and making me Your very own. You know that there are some areas of my life in which I am burdened by a yoke. No one else but You knows how bound up I can be, and I need Your help to get free. Lord, I know that You have already provided everything I need for life and godliness. Please remove the bondages from me that hamper me and hinder me from receiving. Thank You, Lord, for bringing complete freedom to me. I give You all praise and all honor. Help me in the days ahead to continue to step into the new liberty You have provided for me. I want to walk in a way that has eluded me until this moment of freedom which You have provided. Thank You for removing and breaking the yoke that has weighed me down, in Jesus' Name, Amen.

Day 63-For ye know the grace of our Lord Jesus Christ, that, though he was rich, yet for your sakes he became poor, that ye through his poverty might be rich. 2 Corinthians 8:9

I declare I will have more than enough because Jesus became poor at the cross, so that I might be financially supplied, so lack be gone for the Lord is my shepherd, I shall not want in, Jesus Name Amen.

Day 64-"But whatever was to my profit I now consider loss for the sake of Christ." Philippians 3:7

Thank You Jesus for living a sacrificial life. Thank You for the opportunity to sacrifice my life for the kingdom, I've learned that it is also a life of freedom, purpose, and meaning. Holy Spirit Thank You for leading and guiding me so I may see Jesus' life lived fully through me in the Name of the Father, Son, and Holy Spirit, Amen.

Day 65-...God who separated me from my mother's womb and called me through His grace, Galatians 1:15

I declare not only will I bring the Church to the people, but I will also bring the people to the church. Lord You have given me a passion to teach. You have also made me a vessel of Your power, not simply a vessel of words. Your power manifests through the Words You give me which impacts people's lives, in Jesus Name Amen.

Day 66-His master replied, "Well done, good and faithful servant! You have been faithful with a few things; I will put you in charge of many things. Come and share your master's happiness!" - Matthew 25:21

Testing allows one to discover how well a product is made when placed under extreme stress. Under stressful times I discover how well I withstand the pressure and make right decisions regardless of outside influences. In life, I see giving in to pressure in the form of compulsive behavior, withdrawal, anger, abuse, moral failure, and dishonesty, to name just a few manifestations. Jesus, You never yielded to pressure. You never made decisions based on outcome. You always made the right decision. You always performed the same no matter what the circumstance. You lived a life based on absolutes, not circumstances. You never gave in to "situational ethics." As You are so am I in this world. I declare I use pressure to help me see where I am in my maturity and determine my level of future responsibility. I trust the product developer. Jesus have made me to perform well under pressure. Thank You Lord, Amen.

Day 67-For as many as are led by the Spirit of God they are sons of God. - Romans 8:14

I declare that fear has no dominion over me. *Lord You* reserved for me an exceedingly great inheritance. You described the Promised Land as a land of milk and honey. My own Promised Land is the same. I am led by the Spirit and I shall enter in like Caleb. "But because My servant Caleb has a different spirit and follows Me wholeheartedly, I will bring him into the land he went to, and his descendants will inherit it" (Numbers 14:24). In Jesus' Name Amen.

Day 68-The relative in humble circumstances ought to take pride in his high position. - James 1:9

Thank You Father for helping me through humbling circumstances. This a high position because of what You are teaching me in these situations. I know You don't intend for me to stay there; it is merely a stopping place to learn more important things I would not learn otherwise. I press into You Lord and trust You for the outcome to these circumstances, in Jesus' Name Amen.

Day 69-"Whoever finds his life will lose it, and whoever loses his life for My sake will find it." - Matthew 10:39

Lord, everything I possess You own, including me. I surrender my life totally and unreservedly as a living sacrifice. Thank You Father for taking care of me and all the possessions You have made me steward of in Jesus' Name Amen.

Day 70 -"Because those who are led by the Spirit of God are sons of God." - Romans 8:14

I declare I can discern the difference between "good things" and "God-things." There are so many things in which I can be involved, and the more successful I become, the greater the temptations to enter into things where You have not called me.

I remind myself that You are my Help and the reason for my success because I listen, wait, and move only when You tell me to move. Thank You Holy Spirit for keeping me on track, in the name of the Father, Son and Holy Spirit. Amen.

Day 71-"But now you must rid yourselves of all such things as these: anger, rage, malice, slander, and filthy language from your lips."- Colossians 3:8

I declare I count myself buried to sin. "In the same way, count yourselves dead to sin but alive to God in Christ Jesus" (Romans 6:11). Lord You have given me the grace to reckon myself dead to sin. Thank You for helping me to find new freedom and peace of mind in my relationship with You and others, in Jesus' Name Amen.

Day 72-When I am afraid, I will trust in you. In God, whose word I praise, in God I trust; I will not be afraid. What can mortal man do to me? Psalm 56:3-4 NIV

I declare I will not accept the verdict of my emotions about this situation. I turn to You Lord and I remember what the Word says. I find Your promises that meets my need. And though; in my emotions I may feel fear, in my spirit I trust You. And that trust brings me into security, peace, and confidence that's much deeper than my emotions. My emotions are just like the waves on the surface of the sea, but deep down in my spirit, in the depths of my being, there is settled peace and confidence, In the name of the Father, Son and Holy Spirit Amen.

Day 73-*And Jabez called on the God of Israel, saying, Oh that thou wouldest bless me indeed, and enlarge my coast, and thine hand might be with me, and that thou wouldest keep me from evil, that it may not grieve me! And God granted him that which he requested. 1 Chronicles 4:10*

Thank You Lord; for not being, a respecter of persons. That what You did for Jabez You have also done for me. Thank You for giving me the mind of Christ. (1 Corinthians 2:16), which gives me the ability and wisdom to be a responsible steward over all You bless me with In Jesus' Name Amen.

Day 74-"Now the serpent was craftier than any of the wild animals the Lord God had made. He said to the woman, 'Did God really say, "You must not eat from any tree in the garden"?'" - Genesis 3:1

Thank You God for freedom and boundaries, freedom to manage what You have entrusted to me, boundaries to protect me from evil. These are meant to enhance my life, not hinder it. Lord You have provided everything I need for life. You also entrusted me with responsibility to manage and work it. Even though temptation may come to go beyond those boundaries, I declare I take the way of escape (1 Corinthians 10:13), In Jesus' Name Amen.

Day 75-"Let the morning bring me word of your unfailing love, for I have put my trust in You. Show me the way I should go, for to You I lift up my soul." - Psalm 143:8

Thank You Lord for waking me up this morning to connect with Your love, renew my trust in You, and hear Your directions for my day. I love You Jesus, In the Name of the Father, Son, and Holy Spirit Amen.

Day 76-Christ has redeemed us from the curse of the law, being made a curse for us, for it is written, Cursed is everyone that hangs on a tree. Galatians 3:13

Thank You Jesus for redeeming me from every curse that came upon creation with the fall of Adam. You have redeemed me from sickness, pain, sorrow, depression, poverty and even death. Your work of redemption has saved, healed, and prospered me, because I know my redeemer lives in me, In Your Precious Name, Amen.

Day 77-*And whatever you do in word or deed, do all in the name of the Lord Jesus, giving thanks to God the Father through Him. Colossians 3:17*

Thank You Jesus, because whatever I need in this life, You are my never-ending supply! Whatever situations may arise, Your loving presence is right there with me. I rest in Your love and supply. My time with You is filled with love, peace, restoration, laughter, grace and gratitude. I am Thankful for You Jesus, Amen

Day 78-*"Now, He who knew no sin was made to be sin for us that we would be made the righteousness of God in Him."* —2 Corinthians 5:21

Thank You Jesus for taking all of my sins and nailing them to the cross. It's all about You and what You've done. Thank You for paying the price for this awesome gift. Realizing that I am the righteousness of God gives me the power to exercise my rights to reign in life. Always in You, Jesus, much love Amen.

Day 79-*"Sanctify them through thy truth: thy word is truth." John 17:17*

Knowledge of Your will is foundational in developing Christian conduct and character. Thank You for the desire to study the scriptures, for The Word reveals Your Will for my actions and attitudes. You have provided all that I need to be successful and victorious in this life. I declare I believe Your Word, Jesus Amen.

Day 80- "That they all may be one; as thou, Abba, art in me, and I in thee, that they also may be one in us: that the world may believe that thou hast sent me." John 17:21

Jesus Thank You for teaching me how to pray, they kingdom come thy will be done in earth as it is in heaven. (Matthew 6:10), I declare and decree in prayer that all Christians are one as You and the Father are one. May we speak the same thing and have no division among us. May we get the revelation that we are one in Christ and one in Spirit and that we experience unity here on earth, In Jesus Name Amen.

Day 81-"Watch ye and pray, lest ye enter into temptation. The spirit truly is ready, but the flesh is weak." Mark 14:38

I declare, I can avoid temptation by avoiding thoughts that generate temptation. In prayer, I have my mind stayed on You Lord and therefore, am not receptive to thoughts that conceive temptation. When not in prayer, I keep my mind on things that are "true," "honest," "just," "pure," "lovely," and a "good report, as Paul mentions in (Philippians 4:8). I focus on the good in every area of my life. Recognizing Your hand in even the smallest things will bring peace and keeps my heart and mind following hard after You Lord Jesus. Amen

Day 82- And God is able to make all grace abound toward you; that you, always having all sufficiency in all things, may abound to every good work: 2 Corinthians 9:8

Jesus, You are my Shepherd, I shall not want. Thank You for Your grace and being my provider. Thank You for making me a thousand time's so many more as I am and blessing me as You promised (Deut. 1:11), so I may abound in every good work. I love You Lord Amen.

Day 83- *And may He be to you a restorer of life and a nourisher of your old age… Ruth 4:15*

Lord, You are outside of time and my faith in You brings me into this timeless zone. Just as You caused Moses to live to 120 with vigor, (Deut. 34:7), and Sarah to receive strength to conceive at 90 (Heb. 11:11), You sent Jesus to be my restorer of life and a nourisher of my old age. Therefore, what the years have stolen will be restored. And even as my years increase, I will not grow weak and weary because the restorer of life and nourisher of my old age is in me! Thank You Lord for everything; In Jesus' Name Amen.

Day 84- *Wherefore be ye not unwise, but understanding what the will of the Lord is. Ephesians 5:17*

Thank You Lord for revealing Your will to me in Your Word. I have removed the limits from You Lord. I no longer evaluate my carnal or outward qualities. I delight myself in You Lord. I am a new person in the spirit, and I can do all things through Christ (Phillippians 4:13). Thy will be done on earth as it is in heaven, in Jesus' Name Amen.

Day 85- ...Have mercy on me O God, according to Thy loving kindness and according to Thy multitude of Thy tender mercies, blot out my transgressions. Wash me thoroughly from my iniquity and cleanse me from my sin. Psalm 51:1-2

Thank You Father for loving me so much. Thank You for Jesus Christ whose blood has washed me thoroughly from all my iniquity and cleansed me from all my sins. Thank You for creating in me a clean heart and renewing a right spirit within me. Thank You for never leaving me or forsaking me. I am so thankful for all that You have done in Jesus' Name I pray, Amen.

Day 86- ...he that comes to God must believe that He is, and that He is a rewarded of them that diligently seeks Him. Hebrews 11:6

Thank You Father that Your Word never comes back void. I declare that I diligently seek You and You have multiplied me as the stars of heaven. You recompense my work (Ruth 2:12), and You reward me good (1 Samuel 24:19). Thank You Lord for all You do, in Jesus' Name Amen.

Day 87- Is anything to hard for the Lord?...Genesis 18:14

I declare that no-thing is too hard for You Lord. You have made me a new creation (2Corinthians5:17), You have healed me from all diseases (Psalm 103:3), You have blessed me as You have promised (Deuteronomy 15:6), and nothing shall by any means hurt me. (Luke 10:19). In Jesus' Mighty Name, Amen.

Day 88- "Be sober, be vigilant; because your adversary the devil walks about like a roaring lion, seeking whom he may devour" 1 Peter 5:8.

Thank You Jesus for defeating the devil. You have taught me that the power he has is temptation and deception. You have also told me that You will keep me in perfect peace as my mind stays on You. Through the power of The Holy Spirit, You keep me alert and watchful against the devil's plots and You have provided a way of escape. All I have to do is submit myself to You and resist the devil and he will flee (James 4:7). I love You Lord, Amen.

Day 89- *But the very hairs on your head are all numbered. Matthew 10:30*

Heavenly Father, this verse lets me know that as long as something concerns me, You have intimate knowledge of me and You never overlook it. You know every small problem I am worried about and every single burden I have. And when I approach You for help, You have all the time for me as if no one else exists. That is how valuable I am to You and how absorbed You are in me! In Jesus' Name Amen.

Day 90- "Do not let any unwholesome talk come out of your mouths, but only what is helpful for building others up according to their needs, that it may benefit those who listen" Ephesians 4:29.

Thank You Lord for giving me strength and wisdom through Your Spirit to think before I speak. The words that come from me are Your words of truth, words of light, words that are appropriate for the moment and the person or people who hear them. Those words are honoring to You and instructional, inspirational, motivational, encouraging to others. I supports others in whatever it is they need, so that they are lifted up and motivated to reach their potential...to glorify You...to be blessed and be a blessing. Thank you for hearing me, Lord. In the name of Jesus, Amen.

Day 91- If any of you lack wisdom, let him ask of God, that gives to all men liberally, and find fault with, and it shall be given him. James 1:5

I declare I will not fret over life's circumstances. Thank You Father for reminding me that I have wisdom because I have the mind of Christ (1Corinthians 2:16). Thank You for reminding me that You supply all my needs (Philippians 4:19) and wisdom is just one of them. You are my central focus which affirms my belief in You which is also confirmation of the wisdom You've provided in Jesus' Name Amen.

Day 92- "*For the weapons of our warfare are not carnal but mighty in God for pulling down strongholds...*" *2 Corinthians 10:4.*

Lord, I know that there are evil influences in this world, causing spiritual battles for Christians. Thank You for strengthening my desire to spend time in Your Word that I hide it in my heart and know it in my mind. Thank You for filling me with wisdom and boldness through Your Holy Spirit to be spiritually wise and on guard, ready to resist temptations and break down the strongholds that would keep me from the life You have for me. Thank you, Lord. In Jesus' name. Amen

Day 93- *But He answered and said, "It is written, 'Man shall not live by bread alone, but by every word that proceeds from the moth of God.'" Matthew 4:4*

Thank You Father for the means to get to know You better. As I read the Word my knowledge of You increase. I have experienced healing and restoration by hearing Your Word, because it is life to all that find them and health to all their flesh, (Proverbs 4:22). I thank You for Jesus, the Word, made flesh and lives with us. Thank You for revelation knowledge that I have all I need in the Word, in Jesus' Name Amen.

Day 94- *My soul finds rest in God alone; my salvation comes from him. He alone is my rock and my salvation; he is my fortress, I will never be shaken. Find rest, O my soul, in God alone; my hope comes from him. He alone is my rock and my salvation; he is my fortress, I will not be shaken.* Psalm 62:1–2; 5–6

"Lord, I declare that You *alone* are my hope, my rock, my fortress, and the source of my salvation." And, true enough, when I say that, it becomes true in my experience, In Jesus Name Amen.

Prayers to Command Your Day

Day 95- *Casting all your cares upon Him for He cares for you. 1 Peter 5:7*

I declare I cast all my cares upon You Jesus. Lord, I know that as the object of Your care, You promised to take care of me for the rest of my life. You are not a man that You should fabricate (Numbers 23:19). I trust You because You love me so much that You left heaven to come and die for me. I am never alone and I am cared for, in Jesus' Name Amen.

Day 96- *He shall be like a tree planted by the rivers by the rivers of water that brings forth its fruit its fruit in its season, whose leaf also shall not wither; and whatever he does shall prosper. Psalm 1:3*

Father God, I see myself as one who will not wither, whose health will not fail. I see whatever I do prospering! I see Your vision of me. That vision is always a good vision. Whenever I see my situation through Your eyes, I find that my situation changes because when I see as You see, I allow You to work as the Almighty in my life, In Jesus Name Amen!

Day 97- *If an enemy were insulting me, I could endure it; if a foe were raising himself against me, I could hide from him. But it is you, a man like myself, my companion, my close friend. - Psalm 55:12-13*

Loving those who have betrayed me cannot be accomplished by mustering it up. It can only happen when I die to self so that You Lord can love through me. This is truly one of those acts of identifying with the cross and the betrayal You endured from Judas. I declare I respond in righteousness and overcome it by Your Grace, in Jesus I trust Amen.

Day 98 – *After this manner therefore pray ye. Our Father which art in Heaven, Hallowed be thy name. Thy Kingdom come, Thy will be done in earth as it is in Heaven. Matthew 6:9-10*

Thank You Jesus for prayer to make things on the earth as it is in heaven. This prayer gives me hope for a better world. I declare Your will on earth and I know You want the best for me. I can see that all things are possible to those who believe. I believe You Jesus, Amen.

Day 99 - ... *The joy of the Lord is your strength. Nehemiah 8:10*

I trust You Lord, You are my strength and nothing shall by any means harm or disturb my peace, in Jesus' Name Amen.

Day 100 – *And these things write we unto you, that your joy may be full 1 John 1:4*

Abba Father, the more I understand what Jesus has done for me, joy rises inside of me that I cannot contain. This joy I have helps to overcome any ailment or circumstances that may attack me. Father I thank You for Jesus, Amen.

Day 101- *In thy presence is fullness of joy. Psalm 16:11*

Thank You Father, for Your promise to never leave me nor forsake me. Therefore I am always in Your presence and full of joy, in Jesus' Name Amen.

Day 102- I in them and You in Me, may they be bought to complete unity to let the world know that You sent Me and have loved them even as You have loved Me. John 17:23

I declare and decree that the body of Christ is no longer fragmented. The body corporately represents Christ to the world. Pride, ego and independence are no longer a factor within the body and we are unified in the purposes and will of Christ in Jesus' Name Amen.

Day 103- And the glory which You gave Me I have given them, that they may be one just as We are one. John 17:22

Thank You Jesus for taking my shame and giving me Your righteousness and restoring the glory of the Lord to me. I am praise worthy, honorable, and glorious because of Your constant good opinion of me, in Your Most Holy Name, Amen.

Day 104- The angel said to them, "Do not be afraid, for behold, I bring you good tidings of great joy which will be to all people. For there is born to you this day in the city of David, a Savior, who is Christ the Lord. Luke 2:10-11

Thank You Jesus for being my Savior. You were always there for me even in the darkest periods of my life. You have provided healing, deliverance, wholeness, and provision. I am no longer afraid because You are always with me. Thank You for coming into the world just for me. Amen

Day 105- Blessed are you O, Israel. Who is like you, a people saved by the Lord? He is your shield and helper and your glorious sword. Your enemies will cower before you and you will trample down their high places. Deuteronomy 33:29

Thank You Father, that because of what Jesus did at the cross; the blessings and promises given to Israel are also mine. Thank You Father for the Holy Spirit who helps me to destroy anything that I elevate above You. I declare You reign in my life. Amen!

Day 106-The fear of man brings a snare but whosoever put his trust in the Lord shall be safe. Proverbs 29:25

Thank You Lord that the acceptance of others is no longer important to me. Your love for me, which cast out fear, is more than enough. I trust You and lean not on my own understanding because You direct my steps. (Proverbs 3:5-6) I declare I don't limit You Lord, in Your Most Holy Name, Amen.

Day 107- ...let God arise, when you lift Him up, all His enemies will scatter... Psalm 68:1

I declare I look to You Lord Jesus above all situation in m life and receive all that You have for me. I rest knowing that Your plan will be great for me. I don't struggle or strive to bring my heart's desires to pass because Lord, You are faithful, in Your Holy Name, Amen.

Prayers to Command Your Day

Day 108- Then she said, "Sit still, my daughter, until you know how the matter will turn out: for the man will not rest until he has concluded the matter this day." Ruth 3:18

Thank You Father, that as I rest, You work for me. In fact, when You work, I end up with more. In fact, it's already done. I declare I rest in You Lord and You have worked on my behalf in Jesus' Name, Amen.

Day 109-*The Lord gave the word: great was the company of those who published it. Psalm 68:11*

Father thank You for Jesus, the Word made flesh. Thy word is a lamp unto my feet and light unto my path. (Psalm 119:105) I declare I will declare Your word around the world and be among those who teach it, In Jesus' Name Amen.

Day 110- *And Jesus said unto them. I am the bread of life: he that cometh to me shall never hunger; and he that believeth on me shall never thirst. John 6: 35*

Thank You Jesus for being my source and my provider. I declare that I don't fret or worry about needs or desires. You meet all my deepest needs. Thank You for loving me so much. Amen!

Day 111- *The Spirit of the Lord God is upon me; because the Lord hath anointed me… Isaiah 61:1*

I declare I operate in the gifts and abilities that God has given me. In Jesus' Name Amen.

Day 112- Happy is he that condemneth not himself... Romans 14:22

I declare that I am happy because there is no condemnation to them that are in Christ Jesus. Thank You Jesus for shedding Your blood for the remission of my sins. (Matthew 26:28) Amen.

Day 113- Every man according as he purposed in his heart, so let him give, not grudgingly or of necessity for Go loveth a cheerful giver. 2 Corinthians 9:7

I declare that I am a cheerful giver. I have all sufficiency in all things that I may give to every good work, in Jesus' Name Amen.

Day 114- *And be ye kind one to another, tenderhearted, forgiving one another, even as God for Christ's sake hath forgiven you. Ephesians 4:32*

I declare that I forgive because I am eternally forgiven. Those who have hurt, used, and abused me; I forgive in Jesus' Name Amen.

Day 115- *But the path of the just is as the shining light, that shineth more and more unto the perfect day. Proverbs 4:18*

I declare that I am better every day, in health, wealth, and wisdom, in Jesus' Name Amen.

Day 116- …thou anointest my head with oil; my cup runneth over. Psalm 23:5

I declare that I am anointed and this anointing I have I received from the Spirit of Christ which abideth in me (Job 2:27), in Jesus' Name Amen.

Day 117- Who *satisfies my mouth with good things so that my youth is renewed like the eagle's. Psalm 103:5*

I declare that God renews my youth and strength every day. You have also created in me a clean heart and renewed a right spirit in, in Jesus' Name Amen.

Day 118-*To everything there is a season and a time to every purpose under the Heaven. Ecclesiastes 3:1*

I declare I give myself enough time to achieve goals. Good things take time and effort and building a stronger relationship with You is one of those good things. I focus only on those task that I feel are worthy of my total attention and time in Jesus' Name Amen.

Day 119—*The Son of Man came to seek and save what was lost. Luke 19:10*

Thank You Father that You specialize in finding lost things. You have found the lost sheep when I have felt that I lost my sense of purpose and significance. Lord You restored me. You have found the lost coin which represents any finances I may have lost. Lord You have recovered them. You have found the lost son, thank You Lord for reclaiming me from Satan's hand. I declare that all loses have been reclaimed, recovered and restored in Jesus' Name Amen.

Day 120- *Now thanks be unto God, which always causes us to triumph in Christ, and makes manifest the savour of His knowledge by us in every place. 2 Corinthians 2:14*

I declare I win because I can do all things through Christ which strengthens me in Jesus' Name Amen.

Day 121- *Have not I commanded thee? Be strong and of a good courage; be not afraid, neither be thou dismayed: for the Lord thy God is with thee whithersoever thou go. Joshua.1:9*

I declare I am strong and courageous because You Lord never leave me or forsake me. Therefore I fear not because You are with me and You strengthen and help me, in Jesus' Name Amen.

Day 122- *But the very hairs of your head are all numbered. Fear not therefore: you are of more value than many sparrows. Luke 12:7*

I declare I am valuable to You Father. You gave Your only begotten Son for me. There is no greater love than this. Thank You Jesus for laying down Your life for me, Amen.

Day 123- *Fear thou not for I am with thee: be not dismayed; for I am thy God: I will strengthen thee; yea, I will help thee; yea, I will uphold thee with the right hand of my righteousness. Isaiah 41:10*

I declare I have no fear of falling into sin because God holds me up. Sin no longer has dominion over me in Jesus' Name Amen.

Day 124- But I trusted in thy mercy; my heart shall rejoice in thy salvation. Psalm 13:5

Thank You Father that You are not a man that You should tell untruths (Numbers 23:19). I declare I trust Your Word and Your mercy, in Jesus' Name Amen.

Day 125- *...He calls His own sheep by name... John 10:3*

I declare I matter to You Lord. You know me by name and have a personal love for me. You've even numbered the hair on my head. You meet all my needs and make my life beautiful in Jesus' Name Amen.

Day 126- *By the which will we are sanctified through the offering of the body of Jesus Christ once for all. Hebrews 10:10*

I declare that I am sanctified by the finished work of Jesus. Amen.

Day 127- *Christ hath redeemed us from the curse of the law... Galatians 3:13*

I declare I am redeemed from the curse of poverty, sickness, and disease in Jesus' Name Amen.

Day 128- *For I will restore health unto thee, and I will heal thee of thy wounds, saith the Lord... Jeremiah 30:17*

I declare that I am healed, whole, and fully restored in Jesus' Name Amen.

Day 129-In God is my salvation and my glory: the rock of my strength, and my refuge is in God. Psalm 62:7

I declare that You Lord are my refuge and strength in Jesus' Name Amen.

Day 130- *Buried with Him in baptism, wherein also ye are risen with him through the faith of the operation of God, who hath raised Him from the dead. Colossians 2:12*

I declare that the same power that raised Jesus from the dead dwells in me. I am risen with Christ. Thank You Lord, Amen.

Day 131- *…that ye might be filled with the knowledge of His will in all wisdom and spiritual understanding. Colossians 1:9*

I declare I have the mind of Christ. I have quick understanding and wisdom in Jesus' Name Amen.

Day 132- *And he shall be like a tree planted by the rivers of water, that bringeth forth his fruit in his season; … and whatsoever he doeth shall prosper. Psalm 1:3*

I declare I am prosperous in every area of my life in Jesus' Name Amen.

Day 133- *The Lord is my light and my salvation; whom shall I fear? The Lord is the strength of my life; of whom shall I be afraid? Psalm 27:1*

I declare I do not fear. The Lord is always with and I am powerful in, Jesus' Name Amen.

Day 134 - *...ye were not redeemed with corruptible things as silver and gold...but with the precious blood of Christ. 1 Peter 1:18-19*

I declare that I am God's priceless, purchased possession paid for by the blood of Jesus Christ, Amen.

Day 135- *For whosoever is born of God overcometh the world: and this is the victory that overcometh the world even our faith. 1 John 5:4*

I declare that my faith in the finish work of Jesus causes me to be an overcomer in Christ because He has overcome the world (John 16:33), in Jesus' Name Amen.

Day 136- *And Jesus said unto them, I am the bread of life: he that cometh to me shall never hunger and he that believeth in me shall never thirst. John 6:35*

I declare that Jesus meets my every need. I don't have to be concerned about anything in Jesus' Name Amen.

Day 137- *...like as Christ was raised up from the dead by the glory of the Father; even so we also should walk in newness of life. Romans 6:4*

I declare I am brand new; old things have passed away in Jesus' Name Amen.

Day 138- *I will praise thee; for I am fearfully and wonderfully made: marvelous are thy works; and that my soul knoweth right well. Psalm 139:14*

Lord I declare I am Yours masterpiece. When You look at me You see Jesus. How marvelous are thy works, in Jesus' Name Amen.

Day 139- *But this Man, Jesus, after He had offered one sacrifice for sins forever, sat down at the right hand of God…for by one offering He has perfected forever… Hebrews 10:12, 14*

I declare I am perfected forever because of Jesus' perfect work at the cross. Thank You Father for Your full acceptance and delight in Your Son's work which caused You to be merciful to me. You have promised that my sins and lawless deeds You will no longer remember, in Jesus' Name Amen.

Day 140- *…do not stay in the stronghold. Go into the land of Judah… 1 Samuel 22:5*

I declare I live in the land of Judah which means praise. When life tries to beat me down, I think about Your goodness and what You've done for me, it makes me want to sing and dance. My attitude moves from discouragement to praise, in Jesus' Name Amen.

Day 141- *Finally, my brethren, be strong in the Lord and in the power of his might. Ephesians 6:10*

I declare that I am strong and mighty in God. Every day I put on the whole armor of God and stand against the strategies of the devil, in Jesus' Name Amen.

Day 142- *Now the Lord is that Spirit: and where the Spirit of the Lord is, there is liberty. 2 Corinthians 3:17*

I declare that I live in liberty and am changed from glory to glory by Your Spirit in Jesus' Name Amen.

Prayers to Command Your Day

Day 143- Who redeemeth thy life from destruction; who crowned thee with lovingkindness and tender mercies; Psalm 103:4

I declared that I am Your beloved. Yes, Jesus I know You love me because You laid down Your life for me. Thank You Lord, Amen.

Day 144- But grow in grace, and in the knowledge of our Lord and Savior Jesus Christ. 2 Peter 3:18

I declare that I have the knowledge of God because I have the mind of Christ according to (1 Corinthians 2:16), I am intelligent in, Jesus' Name Amen.

Day 145- I am the good shepherd, and know my sheep and am known of mine. John 10:14

I declare that Jesus, You know me intimately and I know You. Thank You Lord for hearing my prayers, in Jesus' Name Amen.

Day 146- And my soul shall be joyful in the Lord: it shall rejoice in his salvation Psalm 35:9

I declare that the joy of the Lord is my strength. I am full of joy, in Jesus' Name Amen.

Day 147- Being justified freely by his grace through the redemption that is in Christ Jesus. Romans 3:24

I declare that the righteousness of God has manifested in my life. I am justified before You Lord because I believe in Your finish work, Amen.

Day 148- *For ye are buried, and your life is hid with Christ in God. Colossians 3:3*

I declare that Satan has to go through Jesus to get to me. I am hidden in Christ. Amen!

Day 149- *Grace and peace be multiplied unto you through the knowledge of God, and of Jesus our Lord. 2 Peter 1:2*

I declared that I have the knowledge of God and He has multiplied grace to me in Jesus' Name. Amen.

Day 150- *For the promise, that he should be the heir of the world was not to Abraham, or to his seed, through the law, but through the righteousness of faith. Romans 4:13*

I declare that I am an heir of the world because You, Lord keep Your promises. I am the righteousness of God in Christ, in Jesus' Mighty Name Amen.

Day 151- *A wise man will hear and increase learning; and a man of understanding shall attain unto wise counsel. Proverbs 1:5*

Lord, I declare that I pursue and extract Your knowledge Lord that has been made available to me. Through the Holy Spirit I receive wise counsel, Who constantly imparts knowledge to me, in Jesus' Name Amen.

Day 152- *For he satisfieth the longing soul, and filleth the hungry soul with goodness. Psalm 107:9*

I declare that I am abundantly blessed because of Your goodness Lord. I am fully satisfied in Jesus' Name, Amen.

Prayers to Command Your Day

Day 153- *For thou, Lord, wilt bless the righteous; with favour wilt thou compass him as with a shield. Psalm 5:12*

I declare that Your favor covers me like a shield. I am highly favored by You Lord, in Jesus' Name Amen.

Day 154- *For the law of the Spirit of life in Christ Jesus hath made me free from the law of sin and dying. Romans 8:2*

I declare that the Spirit of life in Christ Jesus has made me free. I can't thank You enough for the remission of all my sins, in Jesus' Name Amen.

Day 155- *And their sins and iniquities will I remember no more. Hebrews 10:17*

I declare that all my sins are erased forever. Thank You Jesus for making me the righteousness of God. Amen.

Day 156- *Therefore being justified by faith, we have peace with God through our Lord Jesus Christ: Romans 5:1*

I declare I am the righteous because You Lord declare me to be. Therefore being declared righteous because You said so, I believe it and receive it, in Jesus' Name Amen.

Day 157- *By whom also we have access by faith into this grace where in we stand, and rejoice in hope of the glory of God. Romans 5:2*

I declare I gain entrance to You Father by Jesus Christ. I enter into Your unmerited favor, healing, and prosperity through my faith in Jesus Christ Amen.

Day 158- *And hope maketh not ashamed; because the love of God is shed abroad in our hearts by the Holy Ghost which has been given to us. Romans 5:5*

I declare I know that You love me which brings hope and an earnest expectation of good. I am not ashamed of the gospel of grace, it never disappoints. Thank You Jesus, Amen.

Day 159- *For if by one man's offence dying reign by one; much more they which receive abundance of grace and of the gift of righteousness shall reign in life by one, Jesus Christ. Romans 5:17*

I declare I shall reign in life by receiving the gift of righteousness from Jesus Christ. I will never let go of Your gift to me, in Jesus' Name, Amen.

Day 160- *Now unto him that is able to keep you from falling; and to present you faultless before the presence of his glory with exceeding joy. Jude 1:24*

I declare I trust You Jesus because You are able to keep me from falling. I receive everything that grace has made available through You Jesus, Amen.

Day 161- *...he that raised up Christ from the dead shall also quicken your mortal bodies by his Spirit that dwelleth in you. Romans 8:11*

I declare that I am energized and strong because the Spirit that raised Jesus from the dead dwells in me.

I am the temple of the most high God. Hallelujah. Amen.

Day 162- *Likewise reckon ye also yourselves to be buried indeed unto sin, but alive unto God through Jesus Christ Our Lord. Romans 6:11*

I declare that I am dead to sin and alive in You Lord. Sin has no dominion over me in Jesus' Name Amen.

Day 163- *Behold my servant, whom I uphold; mine elect, in whom my soul delighteth... Isaiah 42:1*

I declare I am God's delight. I am His elect and He chose me. He loves me in Jesus' Name Amen.

Day 164- *There is therefore now no condemnation to them which are in Christ Jesus, who walk not after the flesh, but after the Spirit. Romans 8:1*

I declare that I walk after the Spirit and therefore I am not condemned because the Holy Spirit directs my path, in Jesus' Name Amen.

Day 165- *Ask, and it shall be given you, seek, and ye shall find; knock, and it shall be opened unto you. Matthew 7:7*

Father I know You never intended for me to succeed alone. You have chosen someone to make a contribution into my life. I partake of all the favor and help You direct to my life, in Jesus' Name.

Day 166- *That the communication of thy faith may become effectual by the acknowledging of every good thing which is in you in Christ Jesus. Philemon 1:6*

I declare that the communication of my faith becomes effectual and I acknowledge every good thing in Jesus is also in me. Amen.

Day 167- *Now unto him that is able to do exceeding, abundantly above all that we ask or think according to the power that works in us…Ephesians 3:20*

I declare that I receive overwhelming abundance so I can be a blessing to others. I take my place as a receiver and I give You Lord, Your rightful place as my Giver and Provider in Jesus' Name. Amen.

Day 168- *When Christ, who is our life, shall appear, then shall ye also appear with him in glory. Colossians 3:4*

I declare that Christ is my life. I believe it and receive it. Amen.

Day 169- *I am crucified with Christ: nevertheless I live; yet not I, but Christ liveth in me: and the life which I now live in the flesh I live by faith of the Son of God, who loved me, and gave himself for me. Galatians 2:20*

I declare I am living my life through the life of Jesus. My life depends on Christ, Amen.

Day 170- *The thief cometh not, but for to take, and to murder, and to destroy; I am come that they might have life, and that they might have it more abundantly. John 10:10*

I declare that You came so that I can have Your life to the full till it overflows and nothing of me is left. Just enough is not enough. I manage the overflow. My victory flows from You Lord, in Jesus' Name. Amen.

Day 171- But my God shall supply all your needs according to his riches in glory by Christ Jesus. Philippians 4:19

I declare that I am a steward that manages Your supply. I am honored to put supply where You need it. I am an instrument of Your favor. Thank You Lord for using me as Your steward. Amen.

Day 172- Beloved, I wish above all things that thou mayest prosper ad be in health, even as they soul prospereth. 3 John 1:2

I declare that I am God's beloved. I partake of God's provisions of love, health, wealth, and wisdom in Jesus' Name Amen.

Day 173- Finally, brethren, what so ever things are not false, whatsoever things are honest, whatsoever things are pure, whatsoever things are lovely, whatsoever things are of a good report; if there be any virtue, and if there be any praise, think of these things. Philippians 4:8

I declare I nurture that inner picture that You hung in my heart. I diligently guard the dream that You planted in my heart through prayer and discretion in Jesus' Name Amen.

Day 174- Which of you by worrying can add one cubit to his stature? Matthew 6:27

I refuse to worry. Lord, I declare I have more confidence in Your love and power working for me than the devil's ability to harm me in Jesus' Name Amen.

Day 175- *Keep thy heart with all diligence for out of it are the issues of life. Proverbs 4:23*

Lord I declare You have created in me a clean heart and the power to create the kind of life I want. I am brand new, in Jesus' Name Amen.

Day 176- *Nay, in all these things we are more than conquerors through him that loved us. Romans 8:37*

I declare I am more than a conqueror. Victory is mine, in Jesus' Name Amen.

Day 177- *...beloved of God, called to be saints: Grace to you and peace from God our Source and the Lord Jesus Christ. Romans 1:7*

I declare that I have grace and peace from God the Father and Jesus Christ. Amen!

Day 178- *For I know the thoughts that I think toward you, saith the Lord, thoughts of peace and not of evil, to give you an expected end. Jeremiah 29:11*

I declare Lord that You take care of every area of my life, even the smallest detail. I know, Heavenly Father that You have plans laid out for me. You carefully consider and make plans for every aspect of my life big and small. There is no problem insignificant for You to handle, in Jesus' Name. Amen.

Day 179- A thousand shall fall at thy side, and ten thousand at thy right hand; but it shall not come nigh thee. Psalm 91:7

I declare Lord that my faith in You gives me access into the secret place of the Most High where no evil can touch me. I have no fear living in the end times because You are my refuge and fortress in Jesus' Name Amen.

Day 180- *Behold the fowl of the air; for they sow not, neither do they reap, nor gather into barns; yet your heavenly Father feedeth them. Are ye not much better than they? Matthew 6:26*

I declare Lord that I operate from heaven's economy because I am not of the world's system and You give me the good life straightaway! Father I know the generosity of Your heart and how You want to make me successful in Jesus' Name Amen.

Day 181- *Blessed be the God and Source of our Lord Jesus Christ who hath blesses us with all spiritual blessings in heavenly places in Christ. Ephesians1:3*

I declare I am blessed because I sit in heavenly places with You Lord. I am a partaker of all the heavenly gifts, in Jesus' Name Amen.

Day 182- *Keep me as the apple of the eye, hide me under the shadow of thy wings. Psalm 17:8*

Lord I declare I am the apple of Your eye and the focus of all Your affection. You love me so much, in Jesus' Name Amen.

Day 183- *To the praise of the glory of his grace, wherein he hath made us acceptable in the beloved. Ephesians 1:6*

Lord I declare I am accepted by You. Thank You Jesus for all You did on the cross for me. Without You I am nothing, in Your Most Holy Name, Amen.

Day 184- *And hope maketh not ashamed; because the love of God is shed abroad in our hearts by the Holy Ghost which is given unto us. Romans 5:5*

Lord I declare I will not be put to shame because You love me. You have given me the Comforter to teach me all things and abide with me forever, in Jesus' Name Amen.

Day 185- *But this man, after he had offered one sacrifice for sins forever, sat down on the right hand of God. For by one offering he hath perfected for ever them that are sanctified. Hebrews 10:12, 14*

Lord, I declare that I am both holy and perfect. Not only did Your offering sanctified me and by the same offering I have been perfected in You Jesus, Amen.

Day 186- Blessing *are upon the head of the just: but destruction covereth the mouth of the wicked. Proverbs 10:6*

I declare I expect good things to happen to me because blessings are upon the head of the righteous, in Jesus' Name Amen.

Day 187- I have glorified thee on the earth, I have finished the work thou gaveth me to do. John 17:4

I declare that my sin debt is paid in full because of Your finish work Jesus. The victory is won. My blessings have been bought by Your blood. There is nothing for me to do but believe, that it is finished, in Jesus' Name Amen.

Day 188- *And I have given you a land of which ye did not labor, and cities which ye built not, and ye dwell in them; the vineyards and oliveyards which ye planted not do ye eat. Joshua 24:13*

Lord I declare I have a revelation of what I have through Your finish work. Your work brings forth abundance and Your blessing. I expect divine provisions because I am already blessed in Jesus' Name Amen.

Day 189- *Then Jesus put out His hand and touched him saying, "I am willing, be cleansed"... Matthew 8:3*

Lord I declare that it is Your will for me to be healed and whole. In fact You took all my sicknesses and disease on Your own body so I don't have to suffer them today. By Your stripes I am healed (Isaiah 3:5). Amen.

Day 190- Who shall bring a charge against God's elect? It is God who justifies. Romans 8:33

Lord, I declare that Your are not judging me. I am completely forgiven and made righteous before You. I refuse to accept any condemnation and I reject every symptom of the curse that I may see in my circumstances in Jesus' Name Amen.

Day 191- Finally, my brethren, be strong in the Lord and in the power of His might. Ephesians 6:10

Lord, I declare that You are my strength. I rest in Your strength Lord and I see Your power manifesting in my life, in Jesus' Name Amen.

Day 192- *...Grace to you and peace from God our Source and the Lord Jesus Christ. Romans 1:7*

Lord, I declare that You give me preferential treatment that I do not deserve. I depend upon You Lord and take full advantage of Your grace in my life, in Jesus' Name Amen.

Day 193- *Grace and peace be multiplied unto you, through the knowledge of God, and of Jesus our Lord. 2 Peter 1:2*

I declare that grace is multiplied to me. The more I behold You Lord and Your love for me, and confess this love; I see Your grace work for me, in Jesus' Name Amen.

Day 194- *For she said, "If only I can make contact with His clothes, I shall be made well." Immediately the fountain of her blood was dried up, and she felt in her body that she was healed of her affliction. Mark 5:28-29*

I declare by faith that all is and shall be well with me, and I expect to see that. No matter how long I have had the problem, or what the experts say it is, an explosion of healing and restoration is taking place and I will receive what I am believing for in Jesus' Name Amen.

Day 195- *Destruction and life are in the power of the tongue, and those who love it will eat its fruit. Proverbs 18:21*

I declare that every word I speak, builds, restores, heals, and brings delight to those in my life. Lord, I line up my words with Your Words which releases Your power to work in my life, In Jesus' Name Amen.

Day 196- *Now unto Him that is able to do exceeding abundantly above all that we ask or think, according to the power that worketh in us. Ephesians 3:20*

As I pray this prayer, I declare and proclaim my healing, provision, and protection because my heavenly Father's heart overflows with love for me. And when I declare a thing He sanctions and establishes it, in Jesus' Name Amen.

Day 197- *...that He may send, Jesus Christ who was preached to you before, who heaven must receive until the times of restoration of all things... Acts 3:20-21*

Father I declare I will not allow the devil to rob me of my health, marriage, children or finances. Theses blessings were blood-bought and paid for by Your Son. I claim restoration, in Jesus' Name Amen.

Day 198- *...Neither do I condemn you; go and sin no more." John 8:11*

Today I declare I have the gift of no condemnation because Jesus was condemned for all my sins. I believe in Jesus' finished work, Amen.

Day 199- So shall My word be that goes forth from my mouth; it shall not return to me void, but it shall accomplish what I please, and it shall prosper in the thing for which I sent it. Isaiah 55:11

Lord, I declare that when Your Word goes forth in prayer, reading, listening, or teaching, it produces the very effect that the Word promises, in Jesus' Name, Amen.

Day 200- ...And when I see the blood, I will pass over you; and the plague shall not be on you to destroy you when I strike the land of Egypt. Exodus 12:13

I declare that when I plead Your blood Jesus, the destroyer cannot come near me. He cannot touch what is covered by the blood. Jesus, Your blood truly protects and set me free. Amen.

Day 201- ...the righteous of faith speaks... Romans 10:6

I declare I am the righteousness of God in Christ. Jesus I know my declaration brings much pleasure to Your heart because I lay hold of what You suffered and died to give me. I love You Jesus Amen.

Day 202- ...God, who gives life to the extinct and calls those things which do not exist as though they did; Romans 4:17

I declare healing and wholeness in every area of my life. I speak Your Word Lord; this is the way You meant for it to be so I call forth healing and wholeness in Jesus' Name Amen.

Day 203- Therefore I say to you, whatever things you ask when you pray, believe that you receive them and you shall have them. Mark 11:24

I declare I already have whatever I pray for because I am already blessed with every spiritual blessing in heavenly places. Jesus Christ, You came to live in me the moment I received You as my Lord and Savior. I have everything I need in You right now, in Your Most Holy Name, Amen.

Day 204- *In Him we have redemption through His blood, the forgiveness of sins, according to the riches of His grace. Ephesians1:7*

I declare I am conscious of who I am in Christ. Jesus, You took my sin and gave me Your righteousness. Sin has no dominion over me, In Jesus' Name Amen.

Day 205- *Let us therefore come boldly unto the throne of grace, that we may obtain mercy, and find grace in time of need. Hebrews 4:16*

I declare that I speak to my heavenly Father every day. I have no fear approaching You Lord because of Your finished work. You are not counting my sins against me which means you hear and respond to my prayers, in Jesus' Name Amen.

Day 206- *...Take, eat, this is my body. Matthew 26:26 ...Power went out from Him and healed them all. Luke 6:19*

I declare that when I partake of the Holy Communion, I am ingesting Your health Jesus into my body. Jesus I believe that You are the true bread of life who took, cancer, diabetes, heart disease, and any disease that tries to attack my body, so that I can have Your supernatural health. And when I eat of Your body with this revelation, I will have life in abundance and Your health, Thank You Lord, Amen.

Day 207- *For do I now persuade men or God? Or do I seek to please men? For yet if I please men, I should not be the servant of Christ. Galatians. 1:10*

I declare I am not a people pleaser but a God pleaser. Pleasing men causes a snare. I focus on You Jesus and what You have done for me, in Your Most Holy Name Amen.

Day 208- *For precept must be upon precept, precept upon precept, line upon line, line upon line, here a little and there a little: Isaiah 28:10*

I declare I refuse to quit trying. Futility is merely a feeling; I conquer it because I am more than a conqueror in Jesus' Name Amen.

Day 209- *...I will never leave thee, not forsake thee. Hebrews 13:5*

I declare I am not discouraged by others who seem too busy or uncaring to encourage me. I remain focused on where I am going. Aloneness...removes the strain of wrong influence. I know Lord that You are with me, in Jesus' Name Amen.

Day 210- *Knowing that whatsoever good thing any man doeth, the same shall he receive of the Lord, whether he be bond or free. Ephesians 6:8*

A seed is anything I do that benefits another person. I declare I sow seeds into quality soil that produces a harvest in Jesus' Name Amen.

Prayers to Command Your Day

Day 211- He that walketh with wise men shall be wise: but the companion of fools shall be destroyed. Proverbs 13:20

Lord I recognize those You send into my life to inspire and energize me. I declare I acknowledge helpful insights gladly and resist the temptation to become defensive and belligerent. I reward those who have made my goals and dreams come true, in Jesus' Name Amen.

Day 212- Surely He has borne our grief's and carried our sorrows… Isaiah 53:4

I declare I walk in greater health because the One who has surely borne my sicknesses and carried my pains says to me, "I AM wiling be cleansed!" AMEN

Day 213- My son, attend to my words; incline thine ear unto my sayings, For they are life unto those that find them, and health to all their flesh. Proverbs 4:20, 22

Heavenly Father, I declare I attend to Your Word. I incline my ears to Your sayings. I will not let them depart from my eyes. I keep them in the midst of my heart, for they are life and healing to all my flesh, in Jesus' Name Amen.

Day 214- Be not deceived God is not mocked: for whatsoever a man soweth, that shall he also reap. Galatians 6:7

I forbid my body to be deceived in any manner. Body, you will not be deceived by any virus, disease, or germ. Neither will I work against life or health in any way, in the words sown to me and by me, in Jesus' Name Amen.

Day 215- Be not deceived, evil communication corrupts good manners. 1 Corinthians 15:33

Each person in my life is a current that can take me toward Your assignment or away from it. I declare I don't depend upon the faith of other people. I don't speak doubt and unbelief. I am a believer and I have faith. Father God, You have dealt to every man the measure of faith, in Jesus' Name Amen.

Day 216- *Casting down imaginations and every high thing that exalteth itself against the knowledge of God, and bring into captivity every thought to the obedience of Christ; 2 Corinthians10:4-5*

I thank You Lord that I can bind imaginations and cast them down. I pull down strongholds and every thought that rises up against the knowledge of God. I take captive now, every thought and imagination unto the knowledge of You Christ Jesus, my Lord, Amen.

Day 217- *"LORD, you have assigned me my portion and my cup; you have made my lot secure. The boundary lines have fallen for me in pleasant places; surely I have a delightful inheritance."* Psalm 16:5-6

Lord, I declare I am fulfilling what You have called me to do. I take proactive steps to bless others, which actually applies a Kingdom principle that results in greater blessings to others, the Kingdom of God, and even to me, in Your Name, Amen.

Day 218- *Wherefore lay apart all filthiness and superfluity of naughtiness, and receive with meekness the engrafted word, which is able to save your soul. James1:21*

I declare I just don't read the Word; I implant it in my soul so it can transform my life. Lord, You have changed me from the inside out. You take the image of the Word that is in my spirit and grafts it into my soul as I behold You in The Word. I outwardly express Your image Jesus that I inwardly possess, in Your Most Holy Name, Amen.

Day 219- *What do you imagine against the Lord? He will make an utter end: affliction shall not rise up a second time. Nahum 1:9*

Father God, I declare that You are the Guardian of my life, health, finances, and sleep. Sickness has no dominion over me. Jesus, You took all diseases on Your body at the cross. You are my stronghold in the day of trouble, in Your Righteous Name Amen.

Day 220- *And we beseech you brethren, which know them that labor among you, and are over you in the Lord, and admonish you; and to esteem them very highly in love for their works sake. 1 Thessalonians 5:12-13*

I declare that I have chosen a mentor that increases my faith in You Lord. I learn from the scars of my mentor as well as his/her sermons. I humbly admire my mentor, Jesus Amen.

Day 221- You hear, O Lord the desires of the afflicted; you encourage them, and listen to their cry, defending the parentless and the oppressed, in order that man, who is of the earth, may terrify no more. Psalm 10:17

I declare protection over the United States of America from terrorist here and abroad. I degree, the safety and security of our military as they fight terrorist organizations around the world. The families that have lost loved ones at the hands of terrorist will be comforted, in Jesus' Name Amen.

Day 222-My flesh and my heart may fail, but God is my strength and my portion forever. Psalm 73:26

I declare I don't let the external and physical dictate to me. Lord You are the inner source of life and strength which is not subject to the weaknesses and fluctuations of my body. Though my outward man perishes, my inner man is renewed day by day, in Jesus' Name Amen.

Day 223- *Then spake Joshua to the Lord in the day the Lord delivered up the Amorites before the people of Israel, and he said in the sight of Israel, Sun, stand thou still upon Gibeon, and thou the moon in the valley of Ajalon. And the sun stood still, and the moon stayed, until the people had avenged themselves upon their enemies. Joshua 10:12-13*

Father God You created time and You can multiply it. Joshua was given control over time and You are no respecter of person. I declare, what You did for him You have done for me. It's not too late for things to improve in my life and radically turn around. You are the God of a second chance. I am not controlled by time. By Your Grace I control it, in Jesus' Name Amen.

Day 224- *Nay, in all these things we are more than conquerors through him that loved us. Romans 8:37*

I declare I can do all things through Jesus Christ who strengthens me. I eliminate can't from my vocabulary. I can do anything Your Word says I can do. I submit my thinking to the Word of God and my whole life is changing today, in Jesus' Name Amen.

Day 225- *In God I put my trust: I will not be afraid what man can do unto me. Psalm 56:11*

I declare that nothing is ever as bad as it first appears. Warfare always surrounds the birth of a miracle and I expect miracles. Battle is my opportunity to prove what I believe. The size of my enemy determines the size of my reward. I expect big rewards. The enemy does not define the timing of battle nor the weapons I will use, in Jesus' Name Amen.

Day 226- *So faith comes by hearing, and hearing by the word of God. Romans 10:17*

Lord, I declare that I know You and what You think of me. Knowing Your Word produces faith in me. It is by faith that I receive everything Your Grace has provided, in Jesus' Name Amen.

Day 227- *My covenant will I not break, nor alter the thing that is gone out of my lips. Psalm 89:34*

Father, Your Word shows the good plans and purposes for my life; the plans to prosper and not to harm me. Not only is Your Word eternal and steadfast, it's also reveals Your character and covenant to me, in Jesus' Name Amen.

Day 228- *If you can believe, all things are possible to him that believes. Mark 9:23*

Father Your Word is full of life and power. The Scripture tells me that You and Your Word are one. Whatever You say Lord, Your Word is true, it gives me clear instructions on how to conduct my life and to deal peacefully with men. I declare I don't compromise the instruction of the Word during challenging times, in Jesus' Name Amen.

Day 229- *Forever, O Lord, your word is settled in heaven. Psalm 119:89*

I declare Jesus; You are number one in my life. My attitude toward the Word is an indicator of my relationship with You. Jesus, You are my final authority. What I do with Your Word determines what Your Word can do with me. The Word is an established fact in my life and it bears much fruit, in Jesus' Name Amen.

Day 230- *Blessed is the man you discipline, O Lord, the man you teach from your law. Psalm 94:12*

When I catch myself thinking or going in the wrong direction, You immediately cause Your Word to come to my mind. This causes me to repent and move back into the right direction which is Your best for me. I declare I receive Your Word with meekness, in Jesus' Name Amen.

Day 231- Therefore put away all filthiness and extreme wickedness, and receive with meekness the engrafted word, which is able to save your souls. But be you doers of the word, and hearers only, deceiving your own selves. James 1:18, 21-22

I declare that the Word in my life produces the fruit of salvation. Lord, Your Word daily loads me with benefits. As long as I stay in Your Word, not aborting the process with my own thoughts, the Word will produce fruit, in Jesus' Name Amen.

Day 232- *For I say, through the grace given unto me, to every man that is among you, not to think of himself more highly than he ought to think; but to be soberly, according as God hath dealt to every man the measure of faith. Romans 12:3*

As a born again believer, I declare I do not have a faith problem. I have the faith of Jesus Christ. The Word tells me that every man has been given the measure of faith, even those who have yet to believe. I believe in a God and Savior that I cannot see. I am a believer, and all things are possible, in Jesus' Name Amen.

Day 233- *We having the same spirit of faith, according as it is written, I believed, and therefore have I spoken, we also believe, and therefore speak. 2 Corinthians 4:13*

I declare I have the same Spirit of faith that raised Jesus from the dead living in me. I speak what I believe. My faith moves my tongue and moves all obstacles in my life. There is power in my words, in Jesus' Name Amen.

Day 234- For by your words you shall be justified, and by your words you shall be condemned. Matthew 12:37

I declare I don't speak words that are contrary to the Word of God. I guard my words and they work for me and cause me to enter into what You Lord have provided. I believe You Lord, right now, for more than I've ever believed You for in the past. And I see what I believe come to pass, in Jesus' Name Amen.

Day 235- *And be not conformed to this world: but be transformed by the renewing of your mind, that you may prove what is the good, and acceptable, and perfect, will of God. Romans 12:2*

Renewing my mind is more than reading and memorizing scripture. I am being retrained. Lord, I read the Word to discover Your character, Your promises, and Your view of me. I declare I think like You Lord, in Your Most Holy Name, Amen.

Day 236- *And immediately Jesus stretched forth his hand, and caught him, and said unto him, "O you of little faith, why did you doubt?" And when they came into the ship, the wind ceased. Then they that were in the ship came and worshipped Him, saying, "Of a truth You are the Son of God. Matthew 14:22-33*

I declare that I've gotten out of the boat. I keep my eyes on You Jesus and Your Word to prevent circumstances from trying to drain my faith. There is not a problem with my faith. The challenge is unbelief. I say and see what You see which helps me to pull the plug on unbelief, in Jesus' Name Amen.

Day 237- *And he said unto them, "Take heed what you hear: with what measure you measure, it shall be measured to you: and unto you that hear shall more be given. Mark 4:24*

I declare I pay attention to what I hear, what I allow to enter my thought process. I believe the promise You Lord have spoken over me. What I think about, ultimately determines what I say and what I do. I think on the things concerning You Jesus, Amen.

Day 238- *For all the promises of God in him are yea, and in him Amen, unto the glory of God by us. 2 Corinthians 1:20*

The grace of God has provided forgiveness, righteousness, healing, peace, provision, and protection for me. I declare I answer Your divine "Yes" with my "Amen" of faith. My thinking and perception has lined up with how You see things, in Jesus' Name Amen.

Day 239- *Guard your heart above all else, for it determines the course of your life. Proverbs 4:23*

My heart is just like a garden, it brings forth a harvest of whatever seed has been planted in it. I declare I take heed what I hear and meditate on. I think about the Word because it has great influence on my heart and attitude, in Jesus' Name Amen.

Day 240- *O taste and see that the Lord is good: blessed is the man that trusteth in him. Psalm 34:8*

The Word of God is my spiritual food. It is Your Word that shows me who You are and what You will do. Your Word teaches me who I am. I declare I feed on the Word of God and allow it to nurture me into maturity, in Jesus' Name Amen.

Day 241- The LORD will open the heavens, the storehouse of his bounty, to send rain on your land in season and to bless all the work of your hand. Deuteronomy 28:12

Thank You Father for calling me out of "Egypt" and into the Promised Land You have set aside for me. I declare that You have provided me the ability to derive provisions from the work You have called me to do. Your Word goes on to tell me that faithful is He that calls you, who will also do it, so I don't have to work in my own strength but Yours, in Jesus' Name Amen.

Day 242- *Redeeming the time because the days are evil. Ephesians 5:16*

I declare my life is like a train on the track of success and Lord You are the Conductor. Lord, You give me 24 golden box cars to load up. What I load into those box cars will determine the speed and the distance my train will move toward my next place of accomplishment. You are the only One who makes my life count and all my accomplishments come from You, in Your Name, Amen.

Day 243- *The steps of a good man are ordered by the Lord: and he delighted in his ways. Psalm 37:23*

I declare I pursue and partake of all the blessings You have for me. Father You reward those who seek after You. Movement towards You changes my environment instantly. Thanks for ordering my steps, Amen.

Prayers to Command Your Day

Day 244- Come unto me, all ye that labour and are heavy laden, and I will give you rest. Take my yoke upon you and learn of me; for I am meek and lowly in heart: and ye shall find rest unto your souls. For my yoke is easy and my burden is light. Matthew 11:28-30

Lord, I declare I expect Your help today and not to carry my burdens alone. I am yoked to You Jesus and You will carry the load for me because You care for me. Jesus You carry me when I am weak and overwhelmed. Nothing is too hard for You; the author and finisher of my faith, in Your Most Holy Name, Amen.

Day 245- Solid food is for the mature, who by constant use have trained themselves to distinguish good from evil. Hebrew 5:14

I declare I intentionally expose myself to Your Word. I acknowledge my dependence on Your Holy Word. It is the source of my strength so that I may take territory for the Kingdom of God, in Jesus' Name Amen.

Day 246- For the Word of God is quick and powerful and sharper than any two edged sword, piercing even to the dividing asunder of soul and spirit, and of joint and marrow, and is a discerner of the thoughts and intents of the heart. Hebrew 4:12

I declare I walk in victory because I wield the Word of God as my powerful weapon against the enemy. There is power and life in the Word which helps me take control of my thoughts, in Jesus' Name Amen.

Day 247-So shall they fear the name of the Lord from the west, and his glory from the rising of the sun. When the enemy shall come in like a flood, the Spirit of the Lord shall lift up a standard against him. Isaiah 59:19

I declare I demonstrate Your Lordship Jesus on the Earth. I say with my mouth, things that agree with Your Word. I know who I am and I take authority. Jesus, You have won the victory! I use the Words of God in defense when the enemy comes to attack, in Jesus' Name Amen.

Day 248- *Grace and peace be multiplied unto you through the knowledge of God, and of Jesus our Lord. 2 Peter 1:2*

I declare that I behold You Jesus and I am changed into the same image from glory to glory. As You are so am I in this world. Situations in my life don't look the same. Favor is multiplied in my life, in Jesus' Name Amen.

Day 249-*For the law of the Spirit of life in Christ Jesus hath made me free from the law of sin and dying. Romans 8:2*

I declare that I keep the power of the Holy Spirit on. And with You I overcome the law of sin and death. I rise above sin and my flesh with Your help. I subject myself to the Word of God which helps me not to fall into sin, in Jesus' Name Amen.

Day 250- *For to be carnally minded is death; but to be spiritually minded is life and peace. Romans 8:6*

I declare I am full of life and peace. I renew my mind with the Word of God. I walk in the spirit and set my mind on spiritual things. I think on whatsoever is true, lovely and of a good report, in Jesus' Name, Amen.

Day 251- *To the praise of the glory of his grace, wherein he hath made us accepted in the beloved. Ephesians 1:6*

Abba, I declare I am chosen by You. You have predestinated me to be an adopted child by Jesus to Himself. I am forgiven and loved, in Jesus' Name Amen.

Day 252- *Wisdom is the principle thing; therefore get Wisdom: and with all thy getting get understanding. Proverbs 4:7*

Dear Father God, Thank You for the mind of Christ which is loaded with wisdom. I declare I have the ability to discern differences, in people, environments, opportunities, and moments. Solomon asked for wisdom and You also gave him wealth. Father You are no respecter of persons and what You did for him You have also done for me, in Jesus' Name Amen.

Day 253- *Be ye angry, and sin not: let not the sun go down on your wrath. Ephesians 4: 26*

I declare I am free from the power of anger. I have power over it. I have power, love and a sound mind. I will not act rashly, but choose to listen quickly and speak slowly.

I say to anger: YOU ARE FIRED! Since it doesn't work, achieve or produce for me, I will not continue to employ it. I resolve conflict today and will not go to bed angry.

I will use what remains of my aggressive feelings against the devil, speaking the Word of God and resisting him FIRMLY in my faith. The violent take the kingdom by force, and that's what I'll do today, in Jesus Name. Amen

Day 254- *But my God shall supply your need according to his riches in glory by Christ Jesus. Philippians 4: 19*

I declare I always have enough, because Philippians 4:19 says You shall supply ALL my needs, according to Your riches. I always have enough because My Lord is more than enough. I believe that seeds meet needs. I am a sower; and therefore I am a reaper. Lord You are a multiplier and so am I. I am called to be fruitful and multiply. You are multiplying every good seed that I have ever sown. As I give, You give back to me good measure, pressed down, shaken together and running over, in Jesus' Name Amen!

Day 255- *And this gospel of the kingdom shall be preached in all the world for a witness unto all the nations; and then shall the end come. Matthew 24:14*

Glory to God! Before the end comes, every nation will have an opportunity to hear the good news that Jesus is Lord! I declare I play an important part in Your plan for these last days. I'll get the job done because I am personally committed to being part of Your plan. I will be right in the middle of the battle. You have provided everything I will need to stand and give the world Jesus! I am Your Body in this earth and You have me totally covered, in Jesus' Name Amen.

Day 256-Herein is love, not that we loved God, but that he loved us, and sent his Son to be the propitiation for our sins. 1 John 4:10

Father God, I declare that You love me as much as Jesus. You think precious thoughts about me all the time! I am Your beloved, and You are mine! There is nothing You are holding back from me. You didn't hold back Your best, therefore You won't hold back the rest! I refuse to be condemned. I am forgiven. I reject the thought that You are mad at me or against me. You are for me, and not against me. Your love toward me cannot be stopped, quenched or compromised, in Jesus' Name Amen.

Day 257-*Let us hold fast the profession of our faith without wavering; (for he is faithful that promised;) Hebrew 10:23*

I declare I believe You Lord. I have a covenant with You. I am blessed of the Lord, the Maker of heaven and earth. You're not a man that You would lie. I trust You Lord Amen.

Day 258- *There shall no evil befall thee, neither shall any plague come nigh thy dwelling. Psalm 91:10*

I believe that no plague, sickness or disease, is coming near my dwelling. I am the healed of the Lord. Thank You Lord I have health. I have strength. I am doing Your will, in Jesus' Name Amen.

Day 259-Wherefore take unto you the whole armour of God, that ye may be able to withstand in the evil day, and having done all, to stand. Stand therefore, having your loins girt about with truth, and having on the breastplate of righteous; and your feet shod with the preparation of the gospel of peace; Above all, taking the shield of faith, wherewith ye shall be able to quench all the fiery darts of the wicked. And take the helmet of salvation, and the sword of the Spirit, which is the word of God: Praying always with all prayer and supplication in the Spirit, and watching thereunto with all perseverance and supplication for all saints; Ephesians. 6:13-18

I declare that You Lord have provided everything I need to live that overcoming life. You have provided for my offense as well as my defense. Your divine power has been given to me. You have not left me unequipped in Jesus' Name Amen.

Day 260- *Make no friendship with an angry man; and with a furious man thou shalt not go: Lest thou learn his ways, and get a snare to thy soul. Proverbs 22: 24-25*

I declare I have godly friendships that add and multiply my life. As a child of God I know my worth. Jesus, You taught me that truth by dying on the cross for me. Access into my life is a gift that is earned, in Jesus' Name Amen.

Day 261- *The Lord God hath given me the tongue of the learned, that I should know how to speak a word in season to him that is weary: he wakeneth morning by morning, he wakeneth mine ear to hear as the learned. Isaiah 50:4*

I declare I speak words of encouragement to those I meet. I am reminded that though I may have encountered criticism, condemnation, and feelings of inferiority, I can plant a seed of life into the lives of others and receive a harvest of Hope, in Jesus' Name Amen.

Day 262- *For my yoke is easy, and my burden is light. Matthew 11:30*

It is easy to live the Christian life, because Christ lives in me. You are at work in me. You are alive in me. You are love in me. I am not alone, and never will be. I am yoked to You, and that's what makes Christianity a relationship with You, rather than a duty for You. I am free, in Jesus' Name Amen!

Day 263- *Therefore thou art inexcusable, O man, whosoever thou art that judge: for wherein thou judge another, thou condemnest thyself, for thou that judge do the same things. Romans 2:1*

I declare I reserve judgment. Things are never as they first appear. I cannot draw conclusions as long as there is missing information. I do not attempt to explain or penalize someone for actions I do not fully understand. Lord. You are the only One with the right to judge and I trust Your judgments, in Jesus Name Amen.

Day 264- *Jesus said unto him, if thou canst believe, all things are possible to him that believeth. Mark 9:23*

I declare I will never be defeated another day in my life. I am redeemed from failure and defeat. I am the head and not the tail. Everything I put my hand to will succeed and prosper. No matter what is against me, I expect the tables to turn to my favor. My faith will not fail, because Jesus is praying for it! Amen!

Day 265- Debate thy cause with thy neighbor himself, and discover not a secret to another. Lest he that hear it put thee to shame, and thy infamy turn not away. Proverbs 25:9-10

I declare I will not share my troubles with someone unqualified to help me. Confidentiality is a gift to be shared in the privacy of prayer or with an intercessor You Lord have assigned to my life. The difference in seasons is who I've chosen to trust. I don't throw away my confidence in Your promises. You will fulfill them, in Jesus' Name Amen.

Day 266- *But ye shall receive power, after that the Holy Ghost is come upon you: and you shall be witnesses unto me both in Jerusalem, and in Judaea, and in Samaria, and unto the uttermost part of the earth. Acts 1:8*

I declare I recognize and honor the Holy Spirit in me. I thank You Lord for the same spirit that raised You from the dead lives in me. I expect Your power to strengthen me to be Your witness. I expect to be led by Your Spirit today, in Jesus' Name Amen.

Day 267- *Let nothing be done through strife or vainglory, but in lowliness of mind let each esteem others better than themselves. Philippians 2:3*

I declare I honor every opinion I hear today. Father, You have authorized all Your children to have a viewpoint and an opportunity to express it. I honor ones right to be heard. I've learned that something I need is often hidden in someone I may not enjoy. When I listen it's the seed that after produces favor, in Jesus' Name Amen.

Day 268- In the body of his flesh through death, to present you holy and unblameable and unreproveable in his sight. Colossians 1:22

I declare that Jesus has declared me Not Guilty. Even when I feel I don't do enough or that I'm not good enough, Lord, You said faith in You is enough. I don't have to fill guilty to be forgive. I am forgiven by faith in You. I stop today, beating myself up about all that I have or haven't done. I rest in the fact that You Jesus are my perfection. I don't have to be perfect. Jesus You already are and I put my faith in You, in Your Most Holy Name Amen.

Day 269- The Spirit alone gives eternal life. Human effort accomplishes nothing. And the very words I have spoken to you are spirit and life. John 6:63

I declare that the Word of God is my strength. It is eternal. I can count on God's Word. Jesus You said, "Heaven and earth will pass away, but My words will never pass away." You have made every promise available to me with the intent to fulfill! I take the Word of God to the bank, in Jesus' Name Amen.

Day 270- God is not a man, that he fabricates, nor a son of man, that he should change his mind. Does he speak and then not act? Does he promise and not fulfill? Numbers 23:19

I declare that You Lord honors Your Word. I don't let Your Word sit on a shelf, I take responsibility for my part to believe the Word and receive what it says is mine. I see the Word as absolute truth. I allow Your Word to teach me and change my perspective. I see what You see and say what You say, in Jesus' Name Amen.

Day 271- *Who is the wise man? And who knoweth the interpretation of a thing? A man's wisdom maketh his face to shine, and the boldness of his face shall be changed. Ecclesiastes 8:1*

I declare that when I smile first I decide the direction the relationship will go. My countenance creates a climate that attracts people toward me. My face telegraphs my attitude toward life, toward others and about myself. The wisdom of You Lord maketh my face to shine, in Jesus' Name Amen.

Day 272- *Howbeit when he, the Spirit of truth, is come, he will guide you into all truth: he shall not speak of himself, but whatsoever he shall hear, that shall he speak: and he will shew you things to come. John 16:13*

I declare I know what the future holds for me because the Holy Spirit tells me of things to come. I expect a fear free life and a fear free future because You Lord have planned a good and perfect future for me. I have not been given the spirit of fear; but I have power, love and a sound mind, to shape my future, in Jesus' Name Amen.

Day 273- *Verily, verily, I say unto you, He that believeth on me, the works that I do shall he do also; and greater works than these shall he do; because I go unto my Father. John 14:12*

I declare that I am not afraid of the devil. All authority in heaven and earth has been given to You Jesus. I walk in just as much authority over the devil as Jesus did. As a joint heir with You Jesus everything that belongs to You belongs to me and I'm jointly responsible for exercising authority over it. Everything is upheld according to Your will and blessing, in the Name of the Father, Son, and Holy Spirit, Amen.

Day 274- *Teach me thy way, O Lord, I will walk in thy truth, unite my heart to fear thy name. I will praise thee, O Lord my God, with all my heart: and I will glory thy name forevermore. Psalm 86:11-12*

Lord, I declare I have total satisfaction in You. It's not You plus something; it's You alone. That's a united heart – when I don't look anywhere but to You Lord for my life, my satisfaction, my peace, in Jesus' Name Amen.

Day 275- *Then said the Lord unto me, Thou hast well seen: for I will hasten my word to perform it. Jeremiah 1:12*

Lord you guard me everywhere I go. I fill my heart and mouth with the good things you say about me. You are watching over Your Word to perform it in my life, therefore I expect something good to happen. I declare I believe in Your promises, in Jesus' Name Amen.

Day 276- *He hath not beheld iniquity in Jacob, neither hath he seen perverseness in Israel: the Lord his God is with him, and the shout of a king is among them. Numbers 23:21*

I declare Lord that You are no respecter of persons. What You have not beheld in Jacob and Israel, You have also not beheld in me. Your grace and mercy are new every morning. My sins, You remember no more because You were punished for my sins in Your body. Jesus, Your righteousness is on my side and in me, in You Righteous Name Amen.

Day 277- *He discovereth deep things out of darkness, and bringeth out to light the shadow of death. Job 12:22*

I declare Lord that You meet me in the depth of darkness. During these times of darkness I am drawn into a great level of intimacy with You where You make spiritual deposits into my life. Lord You reveal deep things in darkness that will be revealed in the light so others can also make withdrawal to aid them in their dark season, in Jesus' Name Amen.

Day 278- *I will instruct thee and teach thee in the way which thou shalt go: I will guide thee with mine eye. Psalm 32:8*

I declare You guide me where I should go with Your eyes. I trust You Lord, I keep my eyes continually on You. Your teaching and instructions are always for my good. Thank You for loving me so much Amen.

Day 279- *For as the rain cometh down, and the snow from heaven, and returneth not thither, but watereth the earth, and maketh it bring forth and bud, that it may give seed to the sower, and bread to the eater. So shall thy word that goeth forth out of my mouth : It shall not return unto me void, but it shall accomplish that which I please, and it shall prosper in the thing whereto I sent it. Isaiah 55:10-11*

Lord, I declare I spend time in Your Word. Your Word strengthens me. Your Word is life to me. You watch over Your Word and it does not return to You void. Your Word shall prosper where You send it. Your Words are the seeds I sow which brings joy and peace, I love Your Word, Amen.

Day 280- Jesus answered and said unto them, Verily I say unto you, if ye have faith, and doubt not, ye shall not only do this which is done to the fig tree, but also if ye shall say unto this mountain, Be though removed, and be thou cast into the sea; it shall be done. Matthew 21:21

I declare I discard thoughts of unbelief and doubt. I don't advertise my doubts but I declare my expectations of a miracle. All things are possible to those who believe, in Jesus' Name Amen.

Day 281- For a testament is a force after men who passed away: otherwise it is of no strength at all while the testator liveth. Hebrews 9:17

Jesus, I declare I see the Bible as Your last will and testament for me. You have placed me in Your will. I don't have to work to find it. Your will is Your covenant toward me. Your promised inheritances are mine through Your blood. Daily I discover what belongs to me and who I truly am, in Jesus' Name Amen.

Day 282- Nevertheless the Lord thy God would not hearken unto Balaam; but the Lord thy God turned the curse into a blessing unto thee, because the Lord thy God loved thee. Deuteronomy 23:5

I declare I expect a turnaround today! No matter how bad it is. Lord You're in the business of turning bad into good. This kind of favor surrounds me like a shield – not because I deserve it but because of what You did for me. You're the only God who raises the dead, so You can turn this around as I trust in You, in Jesus' Name Amen!

Day 283- *In the beginning was the Word, and the Word was with God, and the Word was God. The same was in the beginning with God. John 1:1-2*

I declare I have a loving relationship with the Word of God. The Word of God is a person and His name is Jesus. I see You Lord on every page which brings healing, hope, and help in every area of my life. When I feed on the Word, You bring life and health to all my flesh, in Jesus' Name Amen.

Day 284- *Ye have not chosen me, but I have chosen you, and ordained you, that ye should go and bring forth fruit, and that your fruit should remain: that whatsoever ye shall ask of the Father in my name, he may give it you. John 15:16*

I declare I am blessed because You Lord have called me into a relationship with You. It's all about You Jesus. You have chosen me as the primary instrument for accomplishing Your plan in the earth, I say yes to You Lord, in Your Most Holy Name Amen.

Day 285- *As far as the east is from the west, so far hath he removed our transgressions from us. Psalm 103:12*

I declare I don't hold anything against myself because Jesus, You don't hold anything against me. I deserve to be punished but You Lord took that punishment for me. I reject guilt and self condemnation that the devil tries to put on me. Thank You Father God that guilt does not come from You. Where I have failed, Your mercy triumphs over judgment, in Your Holy Name Amen.

Day 286- For by one man's disobedience many were made sinners, so by the obedience of one shall many be made righteous. Romans 5:19

I declare that I am established in what You, Jesus have done. I am conscience of my everlasting righteousness in You. I reign over sin, bad habits, sickness, and lack and everything that holds me back from a victorious life, in Your Name Lord Amen.

Day 287-Lo, progeny are a heritage of the Lord: and the fruit of the womb is his reward. Psalm 127:3

I declare Father God that I've learned so much from You on how to be a wonderful parent. I non-judgmentally converse with my child. I communicate with the intent to learn and not condemn. My child is a reward from God. I draw my child into a relationship using loving kindness, in Jesus' Name Amen.

Day 288- *But by the grace of God I am what I am: and his grace which was bestowed upon me was not in vein; but I labored more abundantly than they all: yet not I, but the grace of God which was with me. 1 Corinthians 15:10*

I declare that I am unlimited in my ability to grow and change. Lord You are the potter and I am the clay. I am what You say I am. Lord You began a good work in me, and You will finish it. You are making me into something good. I am Your workmanship—Your work of art. You are good at this and has been doing it a long time! I am not in bondage to my weaknesses and former limitations. They do not define me. Every day and every moment that passes is making me more and more like You Jesus Amen!

Day 289- *My little ones, let us not love in word, neither in tongue; but in deed and in truth. 1 John 3:18*

Lord, I declare that You demonstrated Your love by sacrificing Your life on my behalf. That's how I know that love is not a feeling to be described. It's an action requiring that I put something or someone else before my own happiness, wants, and needs, in Your Faithful Name Amen.

Day 290- *Fight the good fight of faith, lay hold on eternal life, whereunto thou art also called, and hast professed a good profession before many witnesses. 1 Timothy 6:12*

I declare I have the victory in life. Jesus, You have won my battle for me. My fight is, to believe. I refuse to stop believing. I walk by faith and not by sight. I'm the head and not the tail. There are ALREADY more for me than those against me. I cast my care and troubles on You Lord. You are fighting for me. You are interceding for me right now! I rejoice in the midst of my battles, no matter what things look like. I choose to praise You, In Your Most Holy Name! Amen.

Day 291- *Hast thou faith? Have it to thyself before God. Happy is he that condemneth not himself in that thing which he alloweth. Romans14:22*

I declare I will never be depressed another day in my life. I decide to stop condemning myself and beating myself up for my shortcomings. Lord, I believe You are working on me every day. I am not a negative thinker. I am positive. You are for me, with me and in me, therefore depression cannot stay. I command every ounce of depression to loose me and let me go, be removed and cast into the sea, In Jesus' Name! Amen.

Day 292- *But the wisdom that is from above is first pure, then peaceable, gentle, and easy to be intreated, full of mercy and good fruits, with partiality, and without hypocrisy. James 3:17*

This world values people who are beautiful, intelligent, strong, and independent. I declare I'm free from pursuing worldly goals and believing conventional wisdom. I defer to others, give to charities, and offer forgiveness. I seek peace and being gentle to others by concentrating on You Jesus and Your finish work. My true worth is defined by my relationship with You: it comes from being Your child, in Jesus' Name Amen.

Day 293- *But seek ye first the kingdom of God, and his righteousness; and all these things shall be added unto you. Matthew 6:33*

I declare when I don't know what to do, I trust You Lord to lead me. I expect You to speak to me. Your still, small voice will be clear to me today. You are my God. You shall supply my every need. I seek the Kingdom of God and Your righteousness, and all the things missing in my life will be added to me, In Jesus' Name! Amen.

Day 294- *Brethren, I count not myself to have apprehended: but this one thing I do, forgetting those things which are behind, and reaching forth unto those things which are before. Philippians 3:13*

I declare what is and what will be with my words. Today I give up the "woulda, shoulda, coulda" mentality. I will not ask "what might have been." I forget what lies behind and refuse to look back anymore at what I missed out on or could have had. I give up regret forever. Lord You have something better for me today, and I accept it, take action toward it, and expect the greatest days of my life ahead- In Jesus' Name! Amen.

Day 295- *If ye abide in me and my words abide in you, ye shall ask what ye will, and it shall be done unto you. John 15:7*

I declare that You Lord answers my prayers. No matter what I see or feel, I walk by faith, and not by sight. Condemnation for my mistakes or shortcomings will not rob me of confidence. You are bigger than my mistakes. Your Word abides in me, and therefore I can ask and receive. I won't be discouraged or give up, because I will reap if I do not faint. It is already done, in Jesus' Name! Amen.

Day 296- *And David enquired at the Lord, saying, Shall I pursue after this troop? Shall I overtake them? And he answered him, Pursue: for thou shalt surely overtake them, and without fail recover all. 1 Samuel 30:8*

I declare I recover all that has been lost, stolen or missing from my life. I have recovered from whatever sin or addiction I've faced. Lord You did it for David, Job; Elijah-You've done it for me. There is always a way, and I receive Your wisdom to find it now. Jesus You came to restore everything back to me as Our Heavenly Father intended. I receive at least double back for everything that I have ever lost, In Jesus' Name! Amen.

Day 297- How God anointed Jesus of Nazareth with the Holy Ghost and with power: who went about doing good, and healing all that were oppressed of the devil; for God was with him. Acts 10:38

I declare I do not deserve the pain and suffering that Jesus already paid the price for. I did deserve it, but Lord You took it; and I refuse to tolerate it or accept it another day in my life. What people have wrongly done to me is not my fault and not my burden to figure out. I am healed from it, by the stripes of Jesus. Father God freely gives me all things, because You did not withhold Your own Son. You love me and desire to bless me with all of the promises of Your Word. You say I DO deserve Your blessings, because I believe in Your covenant, In Jesus' Name! Amen.

Day 298- *My brethren, count it all joy when ye fall into divers temptations. James 1:2*

I declare I am going to make it. I am going to make it emotionally. I am going to make it financially. I am going to make it through everything I'm facing or will face. Lord You brought me this far. You lead me all the way. You have opened a door for me to make it. You will carry me when I'm weary. I will praise my way through this to the way You have provided, In Jesus' Name! Amen.

Day 299- For I say, through the grace given unto me, to every man that is among you, not to think of himself more highly than he ought to think; but to think soberly, according as God hath dealt to every man the measure of faith. Romans 12:3

I declare I don't live below my God-given privileges. I have received faith of the same kind as Christ, because I have the mind of Christ. You have granted me EVERYTHING pertaining to life and godliness. That includes every area of my life, In Jesus' Name! Amen.

Day 300- *For we dare not make ourselves of the number, or compare ourselves with some that commend themselves: but they measuring themselves b themselves, and comparing themselves among themselves, are not wise. 2 Corinthians 10:12*

I declare I focus my prayer and start my day with what You Lord have already done in my life. I will bless the Lord at all times, Your praise, shall continually be in my mouth. I am already complete in You Jesus. I give up comparing myself to others, and I expect You to make up to me all that I have lost through years of backward thinking, In Jesus' Name, Amen.

Day 301- And the Lord God commanded the man, saying, of every tree of the garden thou mayest freely eat: But of the tree of the knowledge of good and evil, thou shalt not eat of it: for in the day that thou eatest thereof thou shalt surely die. Genesis 2:16-17

I declare I eat freely of the Word of God, Your love, and Your grace, and I am satisfied! The Holy Spirit strengthens whatever is weak or lacking in my life. I can make it through anything and live in any condition, because the Anointed One lives in me. You have supplied my every need, giving me all things pertaining to life and godliness. I am not one thing short of being happy. I am blessed, happy, fortunate, and to be envied, because You have favored me, Therefore, I lack no good thing, in Jesus' Name, Amen!

Day 302- *And the Lord shall make thee the head, and not the tail; and thou shalt be above only, and thou shalt not be beneath; if thou hearken unto the commandments of the Lord thy God, which command thee this day, to observe and to do them. Deuteronomy 28:13*

Thank You Jesus for fulfilling the law so I can receive all of the promises. I declare I think of myself the way You think of me: I am the head and not the tail, I am above, not beneath; I am blessed coming in and going out. I deliberately overcome negative thoughts by voicing positive ones from Your Word. I release the spirit of faith in my life by believing and speaking Your Word. I eliminate negative attitudes by commanding them to leave my life. I agree with You Lord that I am victorious in all things and more than a conqueror, in Jesus' Name, Amen!

Day 303- Ask of me, and I shall give thee the heathen for thine inheritance, and the uttermost parts of the earth for thy possession. Psalm 2:8

Lord, I declare I renew my mind to Your language. I give up small thinking. I agree with Your way of looking at things. I decide to think bigger and bigger every day, and to ask for things You said I could ask for. I accept the visions and dreams that the Holy Spirit wants to give to me, and I let go of all fear-based small thoughts. I will not stop dreaming. I will not stop trying. I have divine authority and am seated with Christ in heavenly places. I am bigger than the mountains because I am made in the image of You Lord. I think bigger, dream bigger and expect bigger today. The Greater One lives in me and has given me the power to see His visions and dreams fulfilled in me, in Jesus' Name, Amen!

Day 304- *Hitherto have ye asked nothing in my name: ask, and ye shall receive, that your joy may be full. John 16:24*

I declare I enlarge my capacity to receive. There's so much more Lord that You can give me and do in my life. I can make it further. I can handle much more in life. I expect Your ability to strengthen me. I will not limit You by my previous experiences, but I will remember all the miracles You have already done. I declare "I am strong, in the Lord and the power of His might. I come to You and receive more of whatever I need-and I receive it, in Jesus' Name, Amen!

Day 305-A good man out of the good treasure of his heart bringeth forth that which is good; and an evil man out of the evil treasure of his heart bringeth forth that which is evil: for of the abundance of the heart his mouth speaketh. Luke 6:45

I declare I give up the thought that my words don't matter. My words have power. They bring me life and satisfaction. Lord I will employ Your method of getting things done, by believing and speaking Your Word. I am made in Your image, and therefore my Words bring things to pass. I believe, therefore I speak, and good things comes forth, In Jesus' Name. Amen!

Day 306-*The sower soweth the word. Mark 4:14*

Lord, I declare that my words set the course of my life. I believe the things which I say will come to pass. I use my words as seeds to plant Your will in my life. As I speak Your Word, I give the Holy Spirit room to work in my life and my situation, In Jesus' Name. Amen!

Day 307-*For all the promises of God in him are yea, and in him Amen, unto the glory of God by us. 2 Corinthians 1:20*

Lord, I declare that Your thoughts toward me are supernaturally GOOD. I believe that I can do all things through Christ which strengthens me! All things are possible and all things are going to work in my favor. I leave behind negative thinking beginning today, in Jesus' Name! Amen.

Day 308- The Lord your God hath multiplied you, and, behold, ye are this day as the stars of heaven for multitude. Deuteronomy 1:10

I declare I embrace a mindset of abundance. I refuse to allow excuses to limit me and keep me stuck in my life, spiritually, emotionally or financially. I am the head and not the tail. What I am, on the inside, is where I'm going on the outside—I am getting ahead. My success is in my seed and I DARE to ask BIG and think BIG, in Jesus' Name Amen!

Day 309-*Furthermore then we beseech you, brethren, and exhort you by the Lord Jesus, that as ye have received of us how ye ought to walk and to please God, so ye would abound more and more. 1 Thessalonians 4:1*

I declare I eliminate excuse-making from my thoughts and words. I will no longer excuse or justify mediocrity in my life; I will not allow lack or failure in my life. Lord You have made me a success and I will press on to experience it. I am forgiven and I will not withhold forgiveness from others. You take up my cause and are my greatest support. I believe there is always a way to succeed. I release my faith by asking You Lord, and expecting You to open the door that no man can close, in Jesus' Name. Amen!

Day 310-*So then they which be of faith are blessed with faithful Abraham. Galatians 3:9*

I declare that You Lord are greater than my heart and greater than my mistakes, even though there is wrong in my life. Your blood cleanses me and brings me into Your blessing. I'm blessed with Abraham the believer. I'm redeemed from the curse of negativity and failure. Goodness and mercy will follow me, because the Lord is my shepherd. I expect to receive every good and perfect gift from my heavenly Father, in Jesus' Name. Amen!

Day 311-*Blessed be the Lord, that hath given rest unto his people Israel, according to all that he promised: there hath not failed one word of all his good promise, which he promised by the hand of Moses his servant. 1 Kings 8:56*

I declare I trust You Lord with all my heart, because You have never broken Your promise. Not one of Your words has failed. It is impossible for You to lie. Whatever You have promised in Your Word, Your answer is YES to me because I am in You. I stand on Your promises, one by one, and declare "Amen", "It is so". In Your Name, Amen!

Day 312-*Ah Lord God! Behold, thou hast made the heaven and the earth by thy great power ad stretched out arm, and there is nothing too hard for thee. 1 Thessalonians 32:17*

I declare You Lord are faithful to do what You promised in my life. You will fulfill Your promises which include saving, healing, restoring, and blessing me. You are the same—yesterday, today and forever. I expect Your miracle power in my life today, in Jesus' Name. Amen!

Day 313- *And all these blessings shall come on thee, and overtake thee, if thou shalt hearken unto the voice of the Lord thy God. Deuteronomy 28:2*

I believe that obeying You Lord will result in my good success. I declare that the wealth being hoarded by this world is coming to me, as I walk by faith. I refuse to stop serving You Lord and acting on Your Word—Your promises are coming to me. You are a rewarder of those who seek You, and I am seeking You, NOW, in Jesus' Name. Amen!

Day 314- *Yea, though I walk through the valley of the shadow of death, I will fear no evil: for thou art with me; thy rod and thy staff they comfort me. Psalm 23:4*

I declare I am not separated from You Lord. I don't have to earn closeness with You. It is a gift. I am IN YOUR PRESENCE and YOU ARE IN ME. In You, I live and move and have my being. I live in this reality. I stop thinking that "God is there, and I am here." You are in my life and my situation right now. No matter what I walk through, I am not afraid—for You ARE with me. I reject the lie that You are out there somewhere. I accept that there is no separation between You and me. (Romans 8:38-39) says, "Nothing can separate me from the love of God!" In Jesus Name, Amen!

Day 315- *But Jesus beheld them, and said unto them, With men this is impossible; but with God all things are possible. Matthew 19:26*

Lord, I declare I am not alone in the challenges and responsibilities of my life. I am yoked to You. Your yoke is easy and Your burden is light. You sent the Holy Spirit to be my Helper. He lives in me and gives me His strength, encouragement and power.

Lord You know what I'm going through, and You have given me the grace and ability to make it. I have a covenant with You; therefore my battles are Your battles. Nothing is too difficult for You, and all things are possible for me, because I believe. I live life from the strength that You supply in me.

I can do all things through You Christ, who infuses me with Your strength! In Your Most Holy Name, Amen!

Day 316-*There is no fear in love; but perfect love casteth out fear: because fear hath torment. He that feareth is not made perfect in love.* 1 John 4:18

I declare that the Word of God is true whether I feel it or not. Lord You have kept all of Your promises and has never failed. Fear leaves me because I rely on something that can't fail—Your promises. What I fear comes upon me, therefore I will fear ONLY YOU LORD, and You will come upon me! You love me perfectly, and I will not think otherwise, no matter what! You have not given me a spirit of fear, but of power, love and a sound mind, in Jesus' Name. Amen!

Day 317- *For God so loved the world, that he gave his only begotten Son, that whosoever believeth in him should not perish, but have everlasting life.* John 3:16

I declare that my heavenly Father tenderly loves me. Lord You and I are inseparable. You continually call me Your beloved; therefore I will be loved by You today. Nothing can separate me from Your love. I am valuable and priceless to You. I am as valuable to You as Jesus is. I receive Your love by faith, in Jesus' Name Amen!

Day 318- The glory of this latter house shall be greater than the former, saith the Lord of hosts: and in this place will I give peace, saith the Lord of hosts. Haggai 2:9

I declare that no matter what is happening in this world, things are getting better and better for me! Jesus has made me righteous through His blood; therefore, my path is getting brighter and brighter every day. My inner man is being renewed day by day. Evil people may go from bad to worse, but the goodness of You Lord follows me, so I go from good to better, every day. I can celebrate in the presence of my enemies, because my cup runs over, and never runs out! Lord, You have saved the best for last in my life, and my latter days will be better than my former days, in Your Name Amen!

Day 319-*For he hath made him to be sin for us, who knew no sin; that we might be made the righteous of God in him. 2 Corinthians 5:21*

I declare I give up thinking about all that is wrong in my life, and I choose to think about what is right. I am the righteousness of God, through Your blood Jesus. I stand in the presence of my Heavenly Father without guilt, shame, inferiority or condemnation. I awake to righteousness and believe it will lead me to a victorious life. I am a joint heir with You Lord. Abba Father, when You look at me, You see Jesus' blood. Father God, You think of me as a conquering, powerful, and holy daughter/son. I will not think of myself as anything less or more than what You think of me, in Jesus' Name Amen!

Day 320- Thou wilt shew me the path of life: in thy presence is fullness of joy; at thy right hand there are pleasures for evermore. Psalm 16:11

I declare that I reject the thought that anyone can make or break my happiness. I take back control of my life, and I choose to be happy today, because Jesus You are my Lord. I have a rich deposit of joy inside of me. And I release its force every time I open my mouth with praise. The ultimate happiness in life is the assurance that I am loved. And since You love me Lord, I walk in the supreme happiness of life. I am free from condemnation because the happiest Man in the world lives in me, in Jesus' Name Amen!

Day 321- *There hath no temptation taken you but such as is common to man: but God is faithful, who will not suffer you to be tempted above that ye are able; but will with the temptation also make a way to escape, that ye may be able to bear it. 1 Corinthians 10:13*

Lord, I declare that You make a way where there is no way. There is always a way out of feeling trapped. I have Your wisdom and I walk by faith, not by sight. I speak to my situation, "Peace, be still." I expect You to open a door that no man can close. No matter how trapped I feel, I will totally trust You. And You will deliver me, as I call upon Your Name, Jesus, Amen!

Day 322-He that committed sin is of the devil; for the devil sinneth from the beginning. For this purpose the Son of God was manifested, that he might destroy the works of the devil. 1 John 3:8

I declare that the devil IS ALREADY DEFEATED. I walk by faith in the victory that is already mine. I am seated with You Christ FAR ABOVE all the power of the enemy. As You are, so am I, in this world. I accept the royalty that You paid for me to have, and I rule and reign with You over life, in Your Mighty Name Jesus' Amen!

Day 323-*This book of the law shall not depart out of my mouth; but thou shalt meditate therein day and night, that thou mayest observe to do to all that is written therein: for then shalt thou make thy way prosperous, and then thou shalt have good success. Joshua 1:8*

I declare that I am being renewed on the inside by the Word of God, which brings success in every area of my life. My success is created by how I think. Lord I agree with Your thoughts, and I meditate on Your Word day and night. Success follows me. I prosper in my soul and I fill my mind with the richness of Your Word, and therefore it spills over into every area of my life. Like Joseph, I will not allow negative circumstances to determine my success or failure. I AM A SUCCESSFUL and PROSPEROUS PERSON, because You are with me, in Jesus' Name Amen!

Day 324- *The impotent man answered him, Sir, I have no man, when the water is troubled, to put me into the pool: but while I am coming, another steppeth down before me. John 5:7*

I declare I don't make excuses like the lame man at the pool, I own the choices I make. I own the life my heavenly Father wants me to have. I choose to look down at life, rather than look up at it. I see it from Jesus' point of view. I'm bigger than my problem, bigger than the mountain, bigger than any enemy I face today. Greater, larger and more dominant is HE that is in me, than he that is in the world. TODAY IS THE BEST DAY OF MY LIFE, because I have control of the choices I make. I will not stay in a defeated, lonely, sick, depressed condition another day of my life. I focus on the inside. I know the thoughts of victory that I am developing will take care of my outside, in Jesus' Name Amen!

Day 325- *Delight thyself also in the Lord: and he shall give thee the desires of thine heart. Psalm 37:4*

I declare I will not be quiet when I face resistance. My prayers will not be silenced by doubt, fear or opposition. At times when I may feel You are not answering, I will stick to Your Word. As my heavenly Father, You say "Yes" to what You have already promised; therefore, I stand on Your promises in all areas of my life. And I will not be denied. I believe that You Lord want to give me the desires of my heart, and not just my needs. When I face resistance, I will add persistence. Just like blind Bartimaeus I will not give up or give in to my present condition. I will press through the opposition and not be denied. I will not tolerate a present condition of discouragement, sickness, poverty or mediocrity, in Jesus' Name Amen.

Day 326-*Jesus saith unto him, I am the way, the truth, and the life: no man cometh unto the Father, but by me. John 14:6*

I declare that as I pray, I believe things will change; they will improve. I walk by faith, not by sight, and faith finds a way. I THINK AND BELIEVE THERE IS ALWAYS A WAY, even when it seems like there is none. And that way of thinking opens doors for me. Jesus, You are the Way when there is no way. Jesus, You are with me no matter what fire I'm in and no matter what the situation. You have made a way for me. When I feel stuck, I think about one step I can take that will move me toward healing, toward blessing, and toward Your will for my life, in Jesus' Name Amen!

Day 327- *Blessed shalt thou be when thou comest in, and blessed shalt thou be when thou goest out. Deuteronomy 28:6*

Jesus, I declare that You have already blessed me. I cannot be cursed. In You, I have ALL the blessings of the Old and New Testament. Goodness and mercy follows me all the days of my life. Lord Your blessings follow me, chase me down, and overtake me. I don't have to chase after them. I am forever forgiven, therefore I am forever blessed. I expect blessings all the time, in Your Most Holy Name, Amen!

Day 328-For God hath not given us the spirit of fear, but of power, and of love, and of a sound mind. 2 Timothy 1:7

I declare that I am no longer under the control of my emotions. They are under my control. As I fill my mind with good thoughts, they will become good emotions. I can control my emotions by my thought life, and my thought life is surrendered to God's Word. I have self-control, a sound mind, and dominion over my life. And from this day forward, my emotions serve me, rather than control me. I pour my emotions out to You Lord, and I don't need to pour them out to others, in Jesus' Name Amen!

Day 329 -And *every man that hath this hope in him purified himself, even as he is pure. 1 John 3:3*

I declare I attach my hope on You Jesus, my unfailing God. My hopes are up! I eliminate the notion of lowering my expectations. I refuse to accept people's advice to "not get my hopes up." I get my hopes up NOW and I keep them up. Lord I expect Your promises to come to pass in my life today! I look up, expecting to receive the best of what You have for me today. Faith and love are keeping my hope alive and purifies my thoughts. I have unlimited and unhindered hope and expectation, in Jesus' Name Amen!

Day 330-And there came a voice from heaven, saying, Thou art my beloved So, I whom I am well pleased. Mark 1:11

I declare that I am approved by You Lord. I am seated with You Jesus in heavenly places. I am above only and not beneath. I have Your royal blood running through my veins. Jesus, You are my righteousness. I have what it takes. You have put a treasure in me and equipped me with the Holy Spirit and empowered me to be up to any task, I am not inferior to anyone or anything and therefore, I am as bold as a lion, reigning in this life in Jesus' Name Amen!

Day 331-*And the barrel of meal wasted not, either did the cruse of oil fail, according to the word of the Lord, which he spake by Elijah. 1 Kings 17:16*

I declare I set my expectation on being run over with Your blessing. Lord thank You that my cup, my money, my time, and my chances are POURING over in my life. Lord You did it for the widow; You have done it for me. You are my God—the God of more than enough, and I expect it today. I am a giver and I know that whatever I give away will always come back to me in good measure, pressed down, shaken together and RUNNING OVER, in Your faithful Name, Jesus Amen!

Day 332-I am crucified with Christ: nevertheless I live; yet not I but Christ liveth in me: and the life which I now live in the flesh I live by the faith of the Son of God, who loved me and gave himself for me. Galatians 2:20

I declare today to eliminate the thought that I am separated from You in any way. Lord You are an ever-present help in my time of trouble. Your ever-presence brings me help! And I will rest in knowing I am in Your presence. I recognize that You are already in me. That's what makes my faith work. I am not trying to live FOR You; I am living FROM You. Your power is in me. Your presence is in me. Your love is in me. Your faith is in me and nothing can ever separate me from Your love which is in Christ Jesus my Lord, Amen!

Day 333- *Jesus answered and said unto them, This is the work of God, that ye believe on him whom he hath sent. John 6:29*

I declare I refuse to stop believing. My work is to believe on You. I walk by faith and not by sight. I'm the head and not the tail. I cast my cares and trouble on You Lord. You are fighting for me. You are interceding for me right now! I rejoice in the midst of my battles, no matter what things look like. There are ALREADY more for me than those against me. I choose to praise You Lord Amen!

Day 334- *Awake to righteousness, and sin not; for some have not the knowledge of God: I speak this to your shame. 1 Corinthians 15:34*

I declare that I walk in true holiness because I am attached to Your love. Being attached to You Lord repels sin and temptation from me. I am the righteousness of God through Your blood Jesus! My heart awakens each day to Your love, grace, and righteousness Lord. I am walking in Your power, and I am free from the power of sin, in Jesus' Name Amen!

Day 335- *And I will restore to you the years that the locust hath eaten, the cankerworm, and the caterpillar, and the palmerworm, my great army which I sent among you. Joel 2:25*

I declare I will recover all that has been lost in my life. I expect the restoration of lost relationships, lost money, lost hope and lost opportunities. I will not settle for loss and lack. Lord You will avenge me. You will restore what has been stolen from me. I ask You and expect You to avenge me of all that has been lost in my life. I call forth at least a seven-fold return of what has been taken from me, In Jesus' Name Amen!

Day 336- *Now thanks be unto God, which always causeth us to triumph in Christ, and maketh manifest the savour of his knowledge by us in every place. 2 Corinthians 2:14*

I declare I have the victory! Jesus You said, "it is finished." My battle has been won over sin, sickness, Satan, lack, fear, discouragement and all other things. IT IS FINISHED! I can't fail today, because YOUR LOVE IS IN ME, and love never fails. I will never be defeated another day in my life, in Jesus' Name Amen!

Day 337-*The Lord will perfect that which concerneth me: they mercy, O Lord, endureth for ever: forsake not the works of thine own hands. Psalm 138:8*

I declare my Lord, You are faithful to do what You promised in my life. You have fulfilled Your promises which include saving, healing, restoring and blessing me. You are the same yesterday, today and forever. Jesus, You did it all on the cross. You have provided for my every need. You have accomplished the things that concern me. You are watching over Your promises to perform them. You have done it before and You will do it again, in Your Most Holy Name, Jesus, Amen!

Day 338- *Happy is he that hath the God of Jacob for his help, whose hope is I the Lord his God. Psalm 146:5*

I declare I have the fullness of joy and happiness in life, because I am in Your presence. I walk in the supreme happiness of life, knowing that I am loved by You. I refuse to condemn myself, since Your Word states that there is no condemnation in Christ Jesus. Lord You will always help me, and my hope is in You, therefore I am happy, in Jesus' Name Amen!

Day 339- *And he arose, and rebuked the wind, and said unto the sea, Peace, be still. And the wind ceased, and there was a great calm. Mark 4:39*

I declare that You Lord are not the source of my storm, but my shelter in the midst of it. I agree with You Jesus and take authority over the storms of life, and declare Peace in the midst of them. I walk in wisdom by acting on the Word, and I rise above every storm, in Jesus' Name Amen.

Day 340- *But without faith it is impossible to please him: for he that cometh to God must believe that he is, and that he is a rewarder of them that diligently seek him. Hebrews 11:6*

Jesus, I declare that You are my rewarder. I adopt Your thinking on each situation, and You reward me. I fix my eyes on You and You complete my faith. Favor surrounds me, promotion surrounds me, and Your rewards surrounds me, in Your Most Holy Name, Amen.

Day 341- But thou shalt remember the Lord thy God: for it is he that giveth thee power to get wealth, that he may establish his covenant which he sware unto thy ancestors, as it is this day. Deuteronomy 8:18

I declare it's not wrong for me to want more to be a blessing. Increasing me is Your idea Lord. You give me the power to get wealth and I am Your covenant ambassador on the earth. You freely want to give me all good things, in Jesus' Name Amen.

Day 342- *Save now, I beseech thee, O Lord: O Lord, I beseech thee, send now prosperity. Psalm 118:25*

Lord, I declare I surrender anxious thoughts to You. I believe there is a solution to financial challenges. I am convinced that there is a way out. I ask You to send prosperity and I expect that You will. For You generously provides for all my needs. You have given me the power to get wealth. That power is in me; therefore I'm free from anxiety, worry, and fear. I don't have to add blessing to my life. It will follow me as I focus on You and Your Kingdom! In Jesus' Name Amen!

Day 343- Howbeit when he, the Spirit of truth, is come, he will guide you into all truth: he shall not speak of himself, but whatsoever he shall hear, that shall he speak: and he will shew you things to come. John 16:13

I declare I can be certain in uncertain times. I am not connected to the economy of this world. I am connected to God's economy. I live by the system of sowing and reaping. I can be certain about the future by sowing the seeds of my Lord's word. I am lead by Your Spirit. You reveal to me things to come, so I can prepare accordingly and be victorious no matter what comes. Just as You led men and women in the Scripture, You lead me, since You're no respecter of persons. I am called and chosen by You, and therefore, I will not stumble. When I don't know what to do, I will trust the Holy Spirit and allow Him to pray through me-bringing me into Your perfect will no matter what is going on in this world, in Jesus' Name, Amen!

Day 344- *To open their eyes, and to turn them from darkness to light, ad from the power of Satan unto God, that they may receive forgiveness of sins, and inheritance among them which are sanctified by faith that is in me. Acts 26:18*

I declare my faith works because I refuse to hold anything against anyone. As I pray, I choose to forgive because forgiveness is the gateway to answered prayer. I refuse to let the poison of unforgiveness defile me and others around me. I will not let a day go by where I hold bitter feelings in my heart toward anyone. I accept the blood of Jesus as the only way to forgiveness and I extend forgiveness to others through that same blood. I have the power to forgive others through the Holy Spirit in me. I release, this day, every person who I have ever held anything against. I am free and so are they! In Jesus' Name, Amen!

Day 345- *(For we walk by faith, not by sight :) 2 Corinthians 5:7*

Lord I accept that forgiveness is not a feeling. It is a decision. I declare the bitter feelings, the problems, the unanswered prayers to change, beginning today, because of the choice I have made. I forgive by faith, which means that I act on Your Word, and declare my forgiveness out loud. I am pleasing to You, whether I feel something or not. I am forgiven and I am a forgiver! I choose to forgive others (AND MYSELF), BEFORE they change, before they deserve it, and before I feel it. I focus on what You Jesus have done for me, rather than what others have done to me, and therefore, I am free. Thank You Jesus, Amen!

Day 346- *No weapon that is formed against thee shall prosper; and every tongue that shall rise against thee in judgment thou shalt condemn. This is the heritage of the servants of the Lord, and their righteousness is of me, saith the Lord. Isaiah 54:17*

I declare that what others have done to me has no power over me or my future. My future is determined by my choices, including my choice to forgive. What others have done to me cannot hurt me. Nothing shall by any means hurt me. What they meant against me, Lord, You turn around for my good. I expect You to interrupt all plots, weapons, and sins against me. Through forgiveness, I release Your power to convert all wrong against me into good. I believe that my attitude and actions of forgiveness will open up an amazing future for me, in Jesus' name, Amen!

Prayers to Command Your Day

Day 347- Dearly beloved, avenge not yourselves, but rather give place unto wrath: for it is written, Vengeance is mine; I will repay, saith the Lord. Romans 12:19

I declare I refuse to measure what's fair by comparison to others. Lord, I overcome what's right in front of me with Your Word. Jesus, You are with me and in me. What I am facing right now is no match for Your presence. I trust You to right every wrong. You will avenge the wrong that has been done to me. You have turned it around for good. I choose to overcome evil with good. Therefore, no matter how unfair things may have seemed, You will make up for whatever has been lost. You are my abundant compensation. I have a covenant with You, and therefore whatever You did for Abraham, You have also done for me, In Jesus' Name! Amen.

Day 348- *We are hard pressed on every side, but not crushed; perplexed, but not in despair; persecuted, but not abandoned; struck down, but not destroyed. We always carry around in our body the death of Jesus, so that the life of Jesus may also be revealed in our body. 2 Corinthians 4:8-10*

I declare Lord that You have a mission for my life. When adversity comes because of this mission, I view it as preparation. Lord You have given me the grace to walk through this time. I am encouraged because You are with me; for You promised to never leave me or forsake me, in Jesus' Name Amen.

Day 349- Keep thy heart with all diligence; for out of it are the issues of life. Proverbs 4:23

I declare I diligently watch over my heart. I will not be passive or tolerant of Satan's thoughts. I have authority over the devil, and I exercise that authority by speaking Your Word. I fight the good fight of faith by believing what You say, and I refuse to accept anything less than the promises of Your Word. I know You are faithful Lord and I trust that You bring Your promises to pass in my life. I take control over doubt by filling my mind and mouth with Your Word, in Jesus' Name! Amen.

Day 350-*Thy word have I hid in mine heart, that I might not sin against thee. Psalm 119:11*

I declare that I am not going to miss Your will for my life! Your Word is Your Will, and I accept and embrace Your Word as the cornerstone of my life. I AM what Your Word says I am. I have a covenant with You that leads me into the right decisions for my life. You keep me in Your Will, as I keep Your Word in my heart and I am blessed, in Jesus' Name Amen.

Day 351- *My son, attend to my words; incline thine ear unto my sayings. Proverbs 4:20*

I declare that Your Word reveals Your will for me over and over again. I commit my works and my ways to You, and You have caused my thoughts to come into agreement with Your will, (Your Word). I expect to be established today and succeed. I keep Your Word in the midst of my heart, in Jesus' Name Amen.

Day 352- *For I delight in the law of God after the inward man: But I see another law in my members, warring against the law of my mind, and bringing me into captivity to the law of sin which is in my members. Romans 7:22-23*

I recognize that I am in a battle between my spirit and my flesh. I declare I will no longer give into the lie that I'm a fake or a hypocrite. I have my flesh trying to control me; but my sprit truly wants to obey You Lord. I yield today, to my spirit, by yielding to Your Word. Jesus, You have delivered me from the wickedness of my past and my flesh. I am forgiven. Everything in me that doesn't want to obey You IS NOT THE REAL ME. The real me is made in Your image and is more than a conqueror through Jesus Christ my Lord, Amen.

Day 353-*That the communication of thy faith may become effectual by the acknowledging of every good thing which is in you in Christ Jesus. Philemon 1:6*

Even when I've fallen short, sinned and felt like a failure, I declare I am not condemned. According to John 14:20, I am in You Lord and I am free. Lord I know You are patient with me, and will finish what You started. I recognize what You have put in me. When I feel like I don't have what it takes, I realize the greatest power in the universe lives in me! It takes the Holy Spirit.. He is my helper! It takes the mind of Christ, and I have it! I have everything I need and amply supplied for You Lord supplies, and I will never lack what it takes again, In Jesus' Name! Amen.

Day 354- There is no fear in love; but perfect love casteth out fear: because fear hath torment. He that feareth is not made a perfect in love. 1 John 4:18

I declare I reject all forms of fear beginning today. I speak to fear and command it to leave my life and family. I walk by faith and not by sight. I surrender my ears to listen to Your Word, and my eyes to focus on Your promises. I expect You to catch me if I stumble or fall. Therefore, I will not be afraid another day in my life, in Jesus' Name Amen.

Day 355- These things I have spoken unto you, that in me ye might have peace. In the world ye shall have tribulation: but be of good cheer; I have overcome the world. John 16:33

Jesus, I take courage today, because You have overcome the world: therefore I have overcome the world. As You are so am I in this world! I declare I will no longer be a victim of life, but a victor over life. I will happen to life, rather than the other way around! I will force my faith upon the things that happen to me, and they will be changed. I confront trials with joy. I develop peace within, by believing Your Word, no matter what is happening on the outside. I have the power to change my future, by the seeds I have sown. What happens to me will be transformed by what happens in me, in Jesus' Name Amen.

Day 356- What shall we the say to these things? If God be for us, who can be against us? Romans 8:31

Lord Your thoughts toward me are precious. I declare that Your opinion of me is all that matters. You are for me, not against me. EVEN IF people are against me, it doesn't matter. I refuse to give them power over my life. I am under Your power, and I walk in that power. No weapon formed against me shall prosper, because I am the righteousness of God, in Jesus' Name Amen.

Day 357- *Therefore take no thought, saying, What shall we eat? Or, What shall we drink? Or Wherewithal shall we be clothed? Matthew 6:31*

Lord Jesus, You know that my thought life is where the battle is decided. I declare that my thoughts produce power when I speak them out loud. I only speak Your Word. I do not accept thoughts that do not line up with Your Word. I trust You Lord and I believe Your Word, it does not return unto You void, in the Name of the Father, Son and Holy Ghost, Amen.

Day 358-*This is the day which the Lord hath made; we will rejoice and be glad in it. Psalm 118:24*

I declare I create an atmosphere of victory with my words. My faith in You Lord extinguishes all doubt. This faith quenches all the fiery darts of the enemy and propels me into all the possibilities that this day can bring. You have something better for me and I rejoice in it, in Jesus' Name Amen.

Day 359- For there is no respect of person with God. Romans 2:11

Lord, Jabez asked that You bless him indeed. I declare that what You've done for Jabez You have also done for me. That Your hand is always with me and that You keep me from evil. And when evil does come it will not grieve me, in Jesus' Name Amen.

Day 360- *In the beginning was the Word, and the Word was with God, and the Word was God. The same was in the beginning with God. John 1:1-2*

I declare I have a living relationship with the Word of God. Jesus, You are the Word of God and I see You on every page. When I read about Abraham placing Isaac on the altar, I see You as the Father's only Son whom He loves and sacrificed for me. When I meditate and feed on the Word, You bring life and health to all my flesh; You are a Wonderful God, Amen.

Day 361-*But God commendeth his love toward us, in that, while we were yet sinners, Christ perished for us. Romans 5:8*

I declare I don't question Your love for me. I look at the cross as the symbol of Your love for me. While I was still a sinner, Jesus, You demonstrated Your love for me. Thank You for loving me so much. Amen.

Day 362-If ye then, being evil, know how to give good gifts unto your little ones, how much more shall your Father which is in heaven give good things to them that ask him? Matthew 7:11

Jesus when Satan tries to cause me to doubt Your love, I look to You, the perfect gift which chases away all doubt. Abba I know that You are not the kind of Father who wants me sick and defeated, keeps me poor and wanting, refuses to provide for my needs, and denies me blessings. I declare I know how much You love me, in Jesus' Name Amen.

Day 363-*And ye shall know the truth, and the truth shall make you free. Romans 8:32*

Lord, I declare I let the truth of Your Word settle in my heart. When factual situations try to cause feelings of worry, I sense the Holy Spirit bearing witness to the truth of Your Word. The difference between facts and truth, facts change but the truth-Your Word remains, in Jesus' Name Amen.

Day 364-*Now the God of hope fill you with all joy and peace in believing, that ye may abound in hope, through the power of the Holy Ghost. Romans 15:13*

Lord, I declare that I expect Your promises to come to pass in my life. I look to You, Jesus for hope. I fix my eyes on You, Jesus and I receive hope as a gift through the power of the Holy Ghost, Thank You Jesus, Amen.

Day 365- The thief cometh not, but to take, and to murder, and to destroy: I am come that they might have life, and that they might have it more abundantly. John 10:10

Father, open the hearts and minds of those who have lost loved ones to know that it's not You taking their loved ones from them. I am sorry for their lost but it hurts my heart to hear people say that You took someone they loved from them. You came to give life abundantly, not death. You know I have also experienced grief because of the death of loved ones. But Lord You gave me the oil of joy for mourning and the garment of praise for the spirit of heaviness. I declare that those grieving will experience the comfort You promised and that their loved ones are with You, healed and whole, in Jesus' Name Amen.

Day 366 -*What is the kingdom of God like? What shall I compare it to? It's like a mustard seed, which a man planted in his garden, and it grew and became a tree… It's like yeast that a woman mixed into a large amount of flour until it worked all through the dough Luke 13:18-20.*

If the tiniest seed can produce a large tree, and if a little yeast can cause an entire lump of dough to rise, then a little faith is all you need to get started. We're stopped short of great things for God because we're searching for BIG faith. Start with small steps and see the great things God can and will accomplish through you.

A little faith is like a muscle, at first small, but as you work it, it will grow.

Day 367- *For whosoever shall call upon the name of the Lord shall be saved. Romans 10:15*

Jesus, help me!

Receive Jesus as Your Savior

If, after reading these prayers you are thinking about accepting Jesus as your Lord and Savior please read on. Choosing to accept and receive Jesus Christ as your Lord and Savior is the most important decision you'll ever make!

God's Word promises," That if thou shalt confess with thy mouth the Lord Jesus, and shalt believe in thine heart that God hath raised Him from the dead, thou shalt be save. For with the heart man believeth unto righteousness; and with the mouth confession is made unto salvation." Romans 10:9-10 "For whosoever shall call upon the name of the Lord shall be saved" Romans 10:13.

By His grace, God has already done everything to provide salvation. Your part is simply to believe and receive.

Pray out loud: *Jesus, I confess that You are my Lord and Savior. I believe in my heart that God raised You from the dead. By faith in Your Word, I receive salvation now. Thank You for saving me.*

Now that you are born again, there's a brand-new you. 2 Corinthians 5:17 states, Therefore if any man be in Christ he is a new creature: old things are passed away; behold all things are become new.

Welcome to the family!

I Would Like to Hear From You

If you have a testimony to share after reading this book, please send an email to: marytaylor13@comcast.net

Also available from Mary Taylor

Deception to the Nth Degree

A Story Of How To Become Victorious Over Deception

&

Thus Saith the Lord

Inspiration from God

BIBLIOGRAPHY

Scripture references from the King James, NIV, Message, and Amplified Version of <u>The Holy Bible</u>

Printed in the United States
By Bookmasters